Imagine a place of **hidden gems and towering tales** of visionaries, pioneers, artists, and nationally renowned athletes . . . a place of undeniable heritage and incredible spirit. In other words, a place called Hancock that has and will forever showcase pure *sisu*.

Published by the City of Hancock, Michigan

Hancock City Council:
William Laitila, mayor
Lisa McKenzie, mayor pro-tem
Ted Belej
Barry Givens
John S. Haeussler
Jeremie R. Moore
John Slivon

Hancock Sesquicentennial Committee:
John S. Haeussler, chairperson
Glenn Anderson
Roland Burgan
Jack Eberhard
Charles Eshbach
Robert Grame
Mary Pekkala
Rob Roy

ISBN-13 9780578117546

Editors: Laura Mahon & John S. Haeussler

Design: Robert Grame, creative director
           Kelsey Norz and Audrey Small, contributing designers

Printed and bound in the USA by Book Concern Printers,
Hancock, Michigan 49930

Edited by Laura Mahon & John S. Haeussler
Creative Direction by Robert Grame

RANDY —

This is a little something that's been
keeping me busy. I hope that you
enjoy it! — JOHN
APRIL 2013

A Hancock, Michigan Anthology

Hidden Gems and Towering Tales

The City of Hancock and the Hancock Sesquicentennial Committee wish to thank the following sponsors who have helped make the sesquicentennial celebration possible through their generous donations:

BIG LOUIE CLUB SPONSORS ($1500+)
Finlandia University
Michigan Technological University
OHM Advisors
Portage Health
Superior National Bank & Trust
Upper Peninsula Power Company

MAYOR'S CLUB SPONSORS ($1000-$1499)
Phi Kappa Tau - Current and Alumni members since 1957

HANCOCK 1863 - 2013

Sponsors

COPPER CLUB SPONSORS ($500-$999)
Book Concern Printers
Gartners Gallery
John, Megan, Maggie, and Jack Haeussler
Mike and Sharon Lahti
MJO Contracting, Inc.
Northern Mutual Insurance Company
Pat's Foods - Your Hometown Grocery Store
Ramada Waterfront Hancock
Rukkila, Negro and Associates, CPAs, PC
Ken Seaton
Superior Block Co., Inc.
Waste Management
Wickley Agency
Dave and Gladys Wiitanen
Steve Zutter, FA - Edward Jones Investments

SESQUICENTENNIAL CLUB SPONSORS ($150-$499)

Amy J's Pasty & Bake Shop

Glenn, Mary Lou, Stacy, Jacki, and Glenn R. Anderson

Celebrations Bridal and Formal

Dave's bp

Dejavu & Daily Brew – Antiques and Coffee Shop

Eliason Law Office P.C.

Fine Line Tire Inc.

Gino's Restaurant

Hancock Business & Professionals Association

Hancock International Office

Houghton County Medical Care Facility

Sigurds Janners, M.D., P.C.

Jutila Center for Global Design & Business, Finlandia University

Kaleva Cafe

Keweenaw Co-op Natural Foods Market & Deli

William Laitila, Mayor of the City of Hancock

Doug, Lisa, Cameron, Erin, and Molly McKenzie

Memorial Chapel Funeral Home – Neil J. Ahola, manager

Northern Auto

Northland Veterinary Clinic

Northwoods Sporting Goods

opusWeb.com

Mary Pekkala

Quincy Mine Hoist Association

James W. Sarazin, D.D.S., P.C.

Tervo Agency

U.P. Laser Engraving & Gifts

This book is dedicated to the Hancock residents of yesterday, today, and tomorrow.

A Familiar Footpath

by F. X. Clifford

Up the hills from Portage Lake,
Is a little path pedestrians take.
In and around the hills it winds,
Until at last their summit finds.

Across its bed of sand and clay,
Gurgles a brook at constant play.
And green and tall the peppermints grow,
Along the banks of its over-flow.

And this is the half-way, short-time stop,
Before the final lap to reach the top.
A quiet, cool, and refreshing retreat,
With running water at your feet.

Over head spreads the arching sky,
Its rim encircling the hill-tops high.
While up in its vast domain of blue,
The fleecy clouds move slowly through.

And now for a last and toilsome grind,
To mount, which all its travelers find.
But oh! when once the table-land is won—
To turn—and scan the lake—what *fun*!

[Published by the Exposition Press in
1949. Francis X. Clifford was a Houghton,
Michigan, librarian and later a teacher
and principal at the Franklin School near
Hancock. He is remembered fondly by
Quincy Hill historian Mike Gemignani.
'A Familiar Footpath' begins at the
East Hancock Stairway.]

HANCOCK 1863 - 2013

Contents

Welcome to Hancock, Michigan's sesquicentennial publication. Why is a community platted in 1859 celebrating its 150th anniversary in 2013? The first municipal officers were elected in 1863. Having identified that as its point of origin, the city held a centennial celebration in 1963. We continue to honor that timeline.

The Hancock Sesquicentennial Committee was formed in early 2012. Initial discussions resulted in a broad range of ideas for this book. In looking back on Hancock's history we quickly realized that it is the extraordinary people who came here that tell the story and answer the question, "Why did so many people excel in this environment?" We decided to focus on such individuals as opposed to buildings, businesses, events, or organizations. These entities all have merit, and some are included herein, but people are the fabric of any community.

HANCOCK 1863 - 2013

Introduction

Hancock Sesquicentennial
Committee

This book is not a comprehensive overview of Hancock's first 150 years. It's an anthology that attempts to provide a glimpse of Hancock's quality of life, nurtured by the pioneer spirit which came with the first immigrants and still exists today. Some of the individuals included have recognizable names in the Copper Country. Others do not, as what notoriety they achieved came elsewhere. The unifying theme is that all of these people have a connection to Hancock. They have each played a role in shaping our community, and in how others view it.

We focused primarily on stories that have not been told, or have not been identified with Hancock. For every person mentioned there are numerous others waiting to be rediscovered and celebrated. This book is a piece of a much larger picture and, as such, an appendix identifying other known publications relating to Hancock is included.

A thorough citation of sources is not presented. A good faith effort has been made by the authors, committee members, and editors to confirm the content contained herein. A similar effort has been made to obtain permission to publish any material not believed to be in the public domain. Files containing notes and source material for many chapters are available at the Michigan Technological University Archives and Copper Country Historical Collections for researchers and others so interested. All addresses mentioned in the book are Hancock addresses unless noted otherwise.

It is our sincere hope that you will enjoy these tales as much as we have enjoyed bringing them to you and that research on Hancock's history continues well beyond this brief anthology.

"BIG LOUIE" MOILANEN
HEIGHT 8'4" TALL
WEIGHT 460 LBS.
S-806

Hervey C. Parke

Given that Hervey Coke Parke owned a company destined to become part of Pfizer Incorporated, the largest research-based pharmaceutical company in the world, it is only fitting that his father was a physician.

HANCOCK 1863 - 2013

by Kristin Vichich

Dr. Ezra Smith Parke and his wife, Rhoda (Sperry), welcomed their fourth child and third son into the world on December 13, 1827. Of English heritage, with ancestors originating from Bristol, the Parkes had settled into Bloomfield, Michigan, and commenced creating a family. Besides Hervey Coke, the Parkes had two daughters - Cornelia and Sarah Abigail - and three other sons - Francis Asbury, Ira Sperry, and Lyman Curtiss.

By all accounts Hervey was not an overly healthy child. Nevertheless, he attended a private academy in Bloomfield and was sent to Buffalo, New York, to attend a high school there during the winter of 1843-1844. Hervey took employment that spring from Garrett V. Mooney, an upholstery dealer and friend of the Parke family. He remained in Buffalo until the autumn of 1845, when he returned to his home state of Michigan. Hervey briefly became a schoolteacher, teaching privately in Oakland County and in the public schools of West Bloomfield. By 1846, however, he had moved back into the world of business. From 1846 until 1848, Hervey worked as a clerk in the hardware store of George L. Bidwell in Adrian, Michigan, and from 1848 through 1850 he worked as a clerk in the general store of his cousin's husband, Willard M. McConnell, of Pontiac, Michigan. In 1850, Hervey had a recurrence of poor health. Seeking to improve it, he traveled north to the cleaner air and freer spaces of the Keweenaw in Michigan's Upper Peninsula. There, Hervey flourished.

His brother-in-law, Marquis W. Kelsey, worked in area copper mines as a superintendent and postmaster, and Hervey found employment with the North American Mining Company (later purchased by the Cliff Mine), near Eagle River. From 1852 to 1861, Hervey was a cashier and bookkeeper at the Cliff Mine, operated by the Pittsburg and Boston Mining Company. He also was a prominent member of Clifton Grace Church, the first Episcopal church in the Upper Peninsula. In 1861, Parke partnered with William Rainey to begin a retail hardware business in the burgeoning village of Hancock. Known as Parke & Rainey, Hervey was the firm's senior member.

March 10, 1863 was a notable day for Hervey, and for Hancock as well. It was on that day, in the office of William Lapp, that the first village officers were elected, establishing Hancock as a self-governed municipality. With 196 votes cast, Hervey C. Parke was elected to the position of village president. Though he would only hold the office for two years, he was the first person to do so, and it cemented his name in the annals of the future city.

The U.S. Civil War ended in 1865, and so did Hervey's desire to remain in the north. He sold the hardware store and brought his wife and daughters down to Detroit, Michigan. They traveled by water on the *Pewabic*, which collided with the *Meteor* on August 9th, off the coast of Alpena, Michigan, in Lake Huron. The *Pewabic* sank with an estimated loss of over 100 lives. All

He was hailed as a man of good character, being generous, devout, steadfast, honest, and industrious.

members of the Parke family were rescued by the *Meteor*[1] and transferred to the *Mohawk*, which carried them to Detroit.

Very shortly thereafter, Hervey purchased the interest of junior partner Francis H. Conant in the chemist firm Duffield and Conant. They operated briefly as Duffield, Parke, and Company, but changes occurred quickly. George S. Davis entered and Dr. Samuel P. Duffield exited the partnership. The company was officially reorganized as Parke, Davis, and Company, with additional partners, around 1870. The Parke-Davis name was retained for generations, the company eventually being acquired by Warner-Lambert in 1970 and subsequently by Pfizer in 2000. Parke, Davis, and Company was incorporated[2] in 1875, with Hervey owning 836 of 3,278 shares valued at $25 apiece. Parke served as president of the company until his death and saw its capital stock exceed $1,200,000, making him a very wealthy man for his time.

But, Hervey was not just another successful businessman of the Gilded Age. He was a vestryman of St. John's Episcopal Church, and he became a senior warden in 1894. He served as a trustee for St. Luke's Hospital. He was also a confirmed family man. On September 10, 1860, Hervey married Frances A. Hunt, the daughter of James B. Hunt, a former Michigan congressman. Within five years they had three daughters: Sarah Cornelia, Mary Eliza, and Annie. Two sons - Francis and James Hunt - were born after the family's move to Detroit. Frances died in 1868 and Hervey married Mary Melinda Mead on September 25, 1872. They had five more children: Hervey Coke, Jr.; Lyman Mead; Elizabeth; Ira Sperry; and, Marie Louise. Hervey was known for his donations of time, money, and goods - what today might be called "random acts of kindness."

Hervey C. Parke died on February 8, 1899, in La Mesa, California, on a ranch he had purchased seven years before. He was hailed as a man of good character, being generous, devout, steadfast, honest, and industrious. His presidency of the Village of Hancock and his success with Parke, Davis, and Company are a testament to that.

[1] Two days later the *Meteor* was claimed by fire, attributed in part to its hull damage from the collision, and sank near Sault Ste. Marie, Michigan.

[2] The five partners at the time of incorporation were Parke, Davis, John R. Grout, William H. Stevens, and Harry C. Tillman. They were steeped in Copper County connections beyond Parke.

William Lapp
by John S. Haeussler

Hancock's first village officers were elected on March 10, 1863, in the office of William Lapp, then justice of the peace. Lapp was among the victorious candidates, being elected to serve as clerk. This was not the first note-worthy election to occur in Lapp's quarters, however. Michigan Legislative Act 245 of 1861 organized Hancock Township and decreed that "the first election in said Township of Hancock shall be held at the hall of William Lapp."[1] Per instructions of the Legislature, the election was scheduled for May 6, 1861, and inspectors included John C. Ryan and Samuel W. Hill. Unfortunately, the exact location of Lapp's office, which served as Hancock's de facto town hall, is not known. Recent research suggests 111 E. Water Street as a likely candidate.

William Lapp was born in Thüringen, Austria, in the fall of 1826. He studied in Cassel (now Kassel) from 1843 to 1846, where he received a degree in mining engineering. He sided with the revolutionists during the political upheaval in Austria, and throughout Europe, in 1848. Although some gains were made, the uprisings were generally considered a failure and Lapp was among the many that made their way to America in the aftermath.

Lapp arrived in Virginia in 1849 and worked with the Baltimore and Ohio Railroad Company. He moved to Eagle River, Michigan, in 1851, and he spent several years engaged in various aspects of copper mining throughout the region. He was involved in the engineering and construction of the Portage Lake tramways utilized by the Quincy, Franklin, and Pewabic mines.

In the early 1860s he learned the art of candle-making from Benjamin Mason, then candlemaker for the Quincy Mining Company. Lapp opened his own business manufacturing mining candles and cylinder oil, in 1864. His factory may have been located in the ravine west of West Street (now Dunstan Street).

Lapp married Sophia Hafenreffer and they had five children. The Lapps resided at 302 3rd Street (now Harris Avenue). William Lapp died in Hancock, of pneumonia on August 27, 1903, a few months after the community that took its formative steps in his office became a city.

[1] Some later histories of Houghton County state that the first Hancock Township election was held at the Baer Brothers store.

March 10, 1863
by John S. Haeussler

While our community was organizing on March 10, 1863, our nation was coming apart at the seams.

The U.S. Civil War was close to reaching its midpoint. Newspapers of the day recounted recent battles and regional hyperbole was commonplace. The strategic importance of the port city of Vicksburg, Mississippi, "the Gibraltar of the Confederacy," was clear. *The New-York Tribune* reported that there "is no doubt as to our ability to get our forces in the rear of Vicksburg." Meanwhile, *The Confederate Union* of Milledgeville, Georgia, assured that "Vicksburg is a hard nut to crack."

In the nation's capital, President Abraham Lincoln issued the following proclamation, offering amnesty to those absent without leave from the Union Army:

"In pursuance of the 26th section of the act of Congress entitled, 'An act for enrolling and calling out the national forces, and for other purposes,' approved on the 3rd day of March, 1863, I, Abraham Lincoln, President and Commander in Chief of the Army and Navy of the United States, do hereby order and command that all soldiers enlisted or drafted in the service of the United States now absent from their regiments without leave shall forthwith return to their respective regiments.

And I do hereby declare and proclaim that all soldiers now absent from their respective regiments without leave who shall, on or before the 1st day of April, 1863, report themselves at any rendezvous designated by the general orders of the War Department No. 58, hereto annexed, may be restored to their respective regiments without punishment, except the forfeiture of pay and allowances during their absence; and all who do not return within the time above specified shall be arrested as deserters and punished as the law provides; and,

Whereas evil-disposed and disloyal persons at sundry places have enticed and procured soldiers to desert and absent themselves from their regiments, thereby weakening the strength of the armies and prolonging the war, giving aid and comfort to the enemy, and cruelly exposing the gallant and faithful soldiers remaining in the ranks to increased hardships and danger,

I do therefore call upon all patriotic and faithful citizens to oppose and resist the aforementioned dangerous and treasonable crimes, and to aid in restoring to their regiments all soldiers absent without leave, and to assist in the execution of the act of Congress 'for enrolling and calling out the national forces, and for other purposes,' and to support the proper authorities in the prosecution and punishment of offenders against said act and in suppressing the insurrection and rebellion.

In testimony whereof I have hereunto set my hand.

Done at the city of Washington, this 10th day of March, A. D., 1863, and of the Independence of the United States the eighty-seventh."

Elsewhere, a royal union was formed. Albert Edward, Prince of Wales (later King Edward VII), married Alexandra of Denmark (later Queen Alexandra) at St. George's Chapel, Windsor Castle, England. The Archbishop of Canterbury, Charles Longley, performed the service. Queen Victoria, still mourning the death of her husband, wore black.

The 62 cannons, which helped force a Union surrender of that ground, are known to this day as "Ruggles' Battery."

Was Hancock's first structure owned by a Confederate major general?

In 1852, C. C. Douglass resided in a cabin on the slope between Portage Lake and the Quincy Mine. Douglass has been cited as Hancock's first resident and significant land owner. But was his cabin actually owned by Daniel Ruggles, a Confederate war hero who was stationed at Fort Wilkins, near Copper Harbor, Michigan, over 15 years before the U.S. Civil War? Late 19th-century accounts identify a cabin erected in 1846 on Ruggles' mining claim as the original building in Hancock.[1] No records have been located to verify this, however. It's clear that Ruggles had a claim on what is presently known as Torch Lake, near Lake Linden, and this property could have been mistakenly identified as being in Hancock. Did Ruggles also have a mining claim on the north shore of Portage Lake or is his 1846 cabin, as reported from 1883 forward, Hancock's longest running myth?

Daniel Ruggles was born on January 31, 1810, in Barre, Massachusetts.[2] He was a descendant of the DeRuggleys, an English family that fought under Richard the Lionheart during the 12th-century Crusades and held distinguished civil and military positions since the 13th-century reign of Edward I. Daniel's great-great-uncle, Timothy Ruggles, was chairman of the First Colonial (Stamp Act) Congress. Timothy's loyalty to the Crown was not well-received in the colonies, and he fled to Canada with the British during the American Revolution.[3]

Daniel Ruggles attended the U.S. Military Academy at West Point, New York. Upon his graduation on July 1, 1833, he was promoted to brevet second lieutenant. He engaged in multiple battles during the Second Seminole War in Florida.

Ruggles married Richardetta Barnes Mason Hooe[4], great-granddaughter of founding father George Mason IV. Marrying into an old and influential Virginia family would later alter the course of his career and life. He was stationed at Fort Wilkins from May 26, 1844 to August 31, 1845. Ruggles traveled extensively throughout the Copper Country collecting characteristic minerals and geological specimens for the U.S. government. In a report filed from Fort Wilkins on February 26, 1845, and published in the October 1845 issue of *The American Journal of Science and Arts*, he stated:

"I have entered into these details because I regard this region as presenting many striking peculiarities, a knowledge of which will become of great importance as the mines are progressively developed, and which will be found to extend, by practical analogy, to the whole mining region of the northwest . . . I am not aware that any more remarkable instance is found on record where metallic bowlders, of great richness, density, and beauty, have been traced, in a manner so satisfactory, to the parent vein."

Ruggles was assigned to the military occupation of Texas later in 1845, and saw combat in both the early and late stages of the Mexican-American War. He was promoted to brevet lieutenant colonel on September 13, 1847, for gallant and meritorious conduct in the Battles of Contreras and Churubusco, Mexico. He was temporarily reassigned to recruiting service for portions of 1846 and 1847, and it is not known if he returned to the Copper Country during this time[5], or ever.

HANCOCK 1863 - 2013

Daniel Ruggles

by John S. Haeussler
and Tim Seppanen

Ruggles resigned from the U.S. Army on May 7, 1861, and joined in the rebellion against the United States. He attained the rank of major general in the Confederate States Army and earned distinction at the Battle of Shiloh in April, 1862. He is noted for bringing eleven cannon batteries to bear on the "Hornet's Nest," a strongly held Union position, following the failure of many Confederate infantry charges. The 62 cannons, which helped force a Union surrender of that ground, are known to this day as "Ruggles' Battery."

Daniel and Richardetta had four sons. George Mason Hooe Ruggles (1842-1843) died in infancy. Edward Seymour Ruggles (1843-1920) graduated from the U.S. Naval Academy in Annapolis, Maryland. He resigned his commission to join the Confederate Navy and, after serving as a special messenger for Confederate President Jefferson Davis, he attained the rank of major in the Confederate Army. Mortimer Bainbridge Ruggles (1844-1902) was born at Fort Wilkins. He attended the U.S. Naval Academy, but he did not graduate before joining the Confederate Army, in which he achieved the rank of first lieutenant. He was arrested, imprisoned, and eventually pardoned for assisting in the attempted escape of John Wilkes Booth following the assassination of President Abraham Lincoln. Gardner S. Ruggles (1854-1910) was a prominent lawyer in Austin, Texas, and served as a U.S. commissioner (magistrate judge).

As part of the reconciliation efforts following the Civil War, Daniel Ruggles served on the West Point Board of Visitors. He died in Fredericksburg, Virginia, on June 1, 1897, and is buried in the Confederate cemetery there. Buried with him are some unanswered questions. We may never know

if Daniel Ruggles indeed built a cabin in Hancock, or, if he did, if C. C. Douglass ever lived in it. But, we do know that he was a decorated soldier with claims to fame well above his possible connection to Hancock, which has been recounted for the past 130 years.

[1] At least one source states that Douglass lived in Ruggles' cabin, but other publications contradict this. Assuming that they were, in fact, two different cabins, they were near each other on the hillside. This was in Section 25, T55N, R34W, in what is now called Ripley. James A. Hicks, of Detroit, Michigan, purchased all 640 acres of Section 26 from the United States and sold it to the Quincy Mining Company in 1848. A third cabin on the Section 25 hillside in 1852 was home to James Ross, a future Union officer in the Civil War.

[2] Ruggles Lane and Ruggles Lane Elementary School in Barre are named after his family.

[3] Timothy's daughter, Bathsheba Ruggles Spooner, was later the first woman executed by the United States.

[4] Mrs. Ruggles' older sister, Lucy Frances Fitzhugh Seymour Hooe, visited Fort Wilkins for much of 1844, and Copper Harbor's Lake Fanny Hooe bears her name. It is misspelled, as she signed her name *Fannie Hooe*.

[5] Given the dates of his military assignments it is possible that Ruggles participated in erecting a Portage Lake cabin in 1846.

The U.S. Civil War in 1863
by Tim Seppanen

In 1863, Michigan was one of 20 northern states and five border states comprising the United States of America (the "North" or "Union") engaged in a civil war with 11 states that formed the secessionist Confederate States of America (the "South" or "Confederacy"). By this time, the war had already raged on for two years since the initial firing upon Fort Sumter, South Carolina, in April, 1861.

1863 has long been considered the high-water mark of the Confederacy. In April, Robert E. Lee's Army of Northern Virginia, fresh from a stunning victory at Chancellorsville against a Union force twice its size, decided on a second invasion of the North. (His first invasion into Maryland ended with the Battle of Antietam on September 17, 1862, which is considered the bloodiest day in American history.) This second invasion culminated in the devastation at Gettysburg, Pennsylvania, from July 1st to July 3rd. A decisive Union victory, the battle ended with the infamous "Pickett's Charge" and casualties numbered in the tens of thousands on both sides. General George Meade, the latest in a succession of commanders of the Union Army of the Potomac, was unable to follow up on the victory at Gettysburg, and the Confederates managed to straggle southward into Virginia. The Southern Army rebuilt under Lee, but it would never again invade the North, and the war consisted of nearly two more years of defensive fighting in the South, especially Virginia, until the surrender by Lee in April, 1865.

In invading the North, Lee wished to relieve pressure on the besieged southern fortress city of Vicksburg, Mississippi, which controlled the Mississippi River. He hoped to draw troops back east and refocus Union efforts on defending Washington, D.C. This didn't happen. The Northern troops in Mississippi were laid out in 12 miles of siege lines under General Ulysses S. Grant. Supported by Union gunboats on the river, they relentlessly assaulted the city from April through its surrender on July 4th. As the last stronghold to fall on the Mississippi, the Confederacy effectively was cut in half. President Abraham Lincoln famously remarked, "'The Father of Waters' again goes unvexed to the sea."

News of the fall of Vicksburg reaching the Copper Country was related by eyewitnesses. John H. Forster and Orrin W. Robinson (both future members of the Michigan Legislature) recounted that the *Northern Light* steamer rounded Pilgrim Point on Portage Lake "blowing and tooting the whistle" in celebration of the news, all the way to the Smith and Harris dock at the old smelting works. Forster related that "the answering shout that went up from the excited crowd made the very earth tremble."

In all, Michigan sent over 90,000 troops into the Federal Army and Navy during the Civil War, incurring over 10,000 casualties. President Lincoln was reported to have said, "Thank God for Michigan."

Hancock Residents in the U.S. Civil War

by Jeremie R. Moore

The following is a list of men who participated in the U.S. Civil War and designated Hancock as their hometown at the time of their enlistment in the Union Army.

Melvin Barlow[3]	27th Michigan Infantry
Alexander Bohrer[1]	27th Michigan Infantry
Allen Brown[1]	9th Michigan Cavalry
Gustave F. Carlston[3]	29th Michigan Infantry
Wellington F. Carr	27th Michigan Infantry
Mills (or Nills) Christinson[3]	29th Michigan Infantry
Charles M. Coffin[3]	29th Michigan Infantry
George W. Cox	27th Michigan Infantry
Evan Danielson[2,3]	29th Michigan Infantry
George W. Danielson	27th Michigan Infantry
John K. Danielson[3]	29th Michigan Infantry
Carl J. Eidenhohn[3]	29th Michigan Infantry
Carl J. Eskholm[3]	29th Michigan Infantry
Frederick J. Fairbrass	1st Michigan Light Artillery
Thomas P. Felker[1]	27th Michigan Infantry
Holk Flordinand[2,3]	29th Michigan Infantry
(or Ferdinand Herk)	
Jacob Getts (or Goetts)[1]	27th Michigan Infantry
Francis Oscar Green[2,3]	29th Michigan Infantry
Thomas Hartley[1,3]	1st Michigan Light Artillery
Andrew P. (or T.) Hellstead[3]	29th Michigan Infantry
(or Hellerstadt)	
Adolph Henneberg	27th Michigan Infantry
Carl Heystraine[3]	29th Michigan Infantry
(or Carl P. Harristine)	
Jacob Hiltz[1]	27th Michigan Infantry
Carl Hogbery[3]	29th Michigan Infantry
Carl (or F.) Hogland[1,3]	29th Michigan Infantry
Henry A. Kichley	27th Michigan Infantry
Augustus La Bush[1]	27th Michigan Infantry
(or Larush)	
John C. Larson (or Lanson)[3]	29th Michigan Infantry
Godfrey Lawson	27th Michigan Infantry
Otto Lenville (or Linville)[3]	29th Michigan Infantry
Evan Lindeberg[3]	29th Michigan Infantry
John F. Lindeberg[3]	29th Michigan Infantry
Carl Anton Lund[3]	29th Michigan Infantry

James Q. (or T.) McCallum	29th Michigan Infantry
Olof Olander[3]	29th Michigan Infantry
Florian Ossier (or Oster)	27th Michigan Infantry
Carl H. Peterson[3]	29th Michigan Infantry
Benson S. Philbrick	27th Michigan Infantry
George Ranscher[2,3]	29th Michigan Infantry
(or Rougher)	
Edward Roby	27th Michigan Infantry
Narcise St. Sarmie[1]	27th Michigan Infantry
William S. Sandberg[3]	29th Michigan Infantry
Casper Schellman	27th Michigan Infantry
William Shulte	27th Michigan Infantry
Meltier Steinger	27th Michigan Infantry
Andrew Strand (or Straw)[3]	29th Michigan Infantry
Peter Urlander[3]	29th Michigan Infantry
(or O'Lander)	
Issac A. Wallstreine[3]	29th Michigan Infantry
A. P. Westergeer[2,3]	29th Michigan Infantry
(or Westergreen)	

[1] Died during the war.

[2] Deserted.

[3] Enlisted in Hancock and is believed to have been from Hancock, but hometown has not been confirmed.

HANCOCK 1863 - 2013

Samuel W. Hill

by Charles Eshbach

I n the Keweenaw area of Michigan's Upper Peninsula, there is a phrase of respect used by working men in the mining and logging professions. Considered by most to be the ultimate compliment describing one's skills in the rough environment of the north woods, the saying "a good man in the woods" is not readily uttered or earned.

Samuel Worth Hill was such a man. He was a surveyor, mining engineer, map-maker, geologist, superintendent, agent, and general "bull of the woods." A man who earned and demanded great respect during the development of Michigan's copper mining district, Sam was well known from Copper Harbor to Ontonagon.

Sam was born in Starksboro, Vermont, on November 6, 1815. As a young surveyor in 1837, he joined the U.S. Army Topographical Corps of Engineers in Racine, Wisconsin, and was sent to Fort Howard in Green Bay. Sam was given the job of surveying the boundary between Michigan and Wisconsin, and he continued north in the Upper Peninsula of Michigan with the lineal survey of this uncharted wilderness. For six months at a time Sam and his crew were subject to the ravages of the wild. During this period he became interested in the Keweenaw, traveling the 200 miles on snowshoes exploring this unbroken land in the harsh, winter environment.

In 1843, Dr. Douglass Houghton, Michigan's first geologist, was put in charge of a geological survey of the mineral region known as the Keweenaw. He appointed Sam Hill to be his assistant, knowing that Sam was already familiar with the region. Three years into the survey, Dr. Houghton drowned near Eagle River, Michigan, hav-ing just left Sam Hill's camp. This loss was devastating to the survey, and Sam was the only man qualified to finish the report. The survey was resumed in 1847, and Sam presented the final results in Washington, D.C., that winter.

Sam Hill was deeply interested in the mineral resources of the Keweenaw and now directed his efforts in exploring and general mine development. In 1848, he assumed charge of a copper mine which had been worked without success. He prepared a report, including his recommendations, for the owner's consideration. This consulting led to investors placing Sam in charge of mine development. During the next decade he directed the development of several profitable mines. He helped establish the Central and Phoenix mines, and he was the first president and manager of the Copper Falls Mine from 1851 to 1855. Rather than become an investor, he always resigned when the operation became successful. As superintendent of the Quincy Mining Company from 1858 to 1860, Sam engineered the mine and mill operation that resulted in Quincy's long-term profitability.

A workaholic, Sam prepared maps of the Eagle Harbor, Phoenix, Pittsburg and Boston, and Waterbury mines, and published reports on the Copper Falls, Dana, Eagle Harbor, Eagle River, Garden City, Michigan, and North Cliff mines.

In July, 1851, Sam married Susan A. Warren in Ontonagon. They made their home above Eagle Harbor, at the Copper Falls Mine location. Susan was noted for her hospitality and entertained many of Sam's business colleagues who came from out east to inspect their investments, which Sam managed.

He was a surveyor, mining engineer, map-maker, geologist, superintendent, agent, and general "bull of the woods."

Sam made another proposal in 1851 – the deep dredging of the Portage River, which opened ship access to Portage Lake and stimulated Hancock and Houghton, Michigan, to prosperity. In 1859, while working as the agent of the Quincy Mining Company, Sam laid out and platted the town of Hancock.

Sam Hill was rough and sometimes harsh, a "get the job done" engineer type. An honest, unselfish, driven man, he was highly respected. His reports brought big investors and long-term financial commitments of millions of dollars that heightened the rush during this boom period. Along with his temperament, Sam developed an uncivilized foul mouth as frustration or anger often prompted expletives. It was so bad that he gained local celebrity status, causing others to vent their own frustration with the phrase, "What the Sam Hill!" This substitute for cussing soon spread across the nation. His penchant for cursing became a part of his legacy, but it is not the measure of the man who contributed so greatly to the making of the greatest mining boom in the world.

Sam's prowess as a mover and shaker in this boom prepared him for a political career. In 1867-1868, and again in 1871-1872, Sam served as state representative from Keweenaw County, Michigan. His iron will, sharp intellect, and readiness to debate made him a formidable representative in the state capital. During this period, Sam also worked for the North American Mineral Land Company. He conducted surveys of Isle Royale, Michigan, and he published a map of the island in 1876. That winter, Sam prepared a native copper exhibit for the Philadelphia Centennial Exposition and won a special medal of honor.

Samuel Worth Hill died in Marshall, Michigan, on August 28, 1889. He was a pioneering leader in the Keweenaw, helping to transform it from a raw wilderness to a world leader in copper production. *The Portage Lake Mining Gazette* paid him tribute stating, "Wherever he located, as far as it has been possible for him to do, he has obtained and dispersed to his employees the benefits and comforts of home and civilized enjoyments. Comfortable dwellings, good schools, and favorite churches have been provided."

The legend of Sam Hill is woven into our American heritage, and undoubtedly that thread is made of copper.

Mary Chase Perry Stratton

"I was trying to decide what I wanted to do and had gone to spend a week at the lake shore to think the thing over. A piece of paper fluttered along the beach and I picked it up. There was an article printed on it headed, 'Develop the Resources of America.' The article outlined the rich possibilities in our own soil for making the clays for pottery ... Ever since, I have been trying to develop the resources of America by using the clays found in our soil."
— Mary Chase Perry Stratton, *The Detroit News*, 1932

HANCOCK 1863 - 2013

by Stephen Alan Smith

Mary Chase Perry Stratton, one of the most innovative ceramicists in the United States, hails from Hancock. She founded Pewabic Pottery, which produced a distinctive and popular style of ceramic pottery and tile featured in architecture throughout the country. Her work is in museum collections around the world, including the Smithsonian and the Louvre.

Mary Chase Perry was born at 222 Hancock Street on March 15, 1867. This modest wood-frame dwelling, now home to The Celtic Quarter, had an adjoining office where her father, Dr. William Walbridge Perry, physician and surgeon, saw patients. It was one of the few buildings that escaped the April 11, 1869 fire that destroyed most of Hancock.

William Walbridge Perry graduated from the University of Michigan in 1846 and Rush Medical College, Chicago, Illinois, in 1850. While a young man he traveled the world, sailing around Michigan's Keweenaw Peninsula and as far away as Australia. In 1858, he married Sophia Barrett in Superior, Wisconsin. Following the birth of their son Frederick, the Perrys moved to Hancock and rented a home from Ransom Shelden. Gertrude, their second child,

was born there in 1862, followed by Mary Chase, who was named after a close friend of Mrs. Perry.

Mary Chase's early childhood included skating on frozen Portage Lake and climbing Quincy Hill with her father. In 1877, Dr. Perry died. It was a tremendous loss for Mary Chase, who took from her father a strong moral responsibility and great determination. Later in her life, Dr. Perry's books on chemistry and the assaying of ores and metals were rich references for her pottery work.

Within a few years of Dr. Perry's death, Sophia Perry moved her family to Ann Arbor, Michigan. Here, Mary Chase was exposed to a broader culture, and while inspired by her cousins and the collegiate atmosphere, she chafed under her own conservatism. Her cousins were "much more sophisticated than we were. They went to the Unitarian church and painted on Sunday afternoons for amusement, decorating plates with birds and flowers ... I longed to break away from my self-imposed Puritanism, but I would not allow myself to yield to temptation." She remembered that later "on a week day, I did paint a robin on a branch with cherries." Miss

Mary Chase Perry working in Stable-Studio, Detroit.

Perry began formal lessons in art, took correspondence courses, and visited various exhibitions. The family moved to Detroit, Michigan, where Miss Perry received private art lessons and was introduced to the then-popular china-painting. She learned how to mix and apply mineral colors and floral designs to cups and saucers and studied under Franz Bischoff, a well-known china-painter and instructor.

Seeking more formal training, Miss Perry moved to Cincinnati, Ohio, a nexus of ceramics and china-painting. She attended the Art Academy of Cincinnati from 1887 to 1889 where her classmates included Maria Longworth Nichols Storer, founder of Rookwood Pottery. Through the Cincinnati Pottery Club she met seminal artists including Mary Louise McLaughlin, an established author on china-painting; Laura A. Fry, an innovative artist; and, Clara C. Newton. It was here that Miss Perry began experimenting with metallic effects on glazed ceramics.

After moving back to Detroit to complete classes, Miss Perry sojourned to Asheville, North Carolina, where she rejoined her family and opened a china-painting studio. By 1893, she had again returned to Detroit and opened a studio on West Adams Street where she gave lessons, sold glazing products, and continued writing articles for china-decorating magazines. By this time Miss Perry was well-known in china-painting circles, both locally and nationally, and her advice and talents were in demand.

In 1897, Miss Perry began working with Horace James Caulkins, a pioneer in the development of high-heat kilns for dental porcelain—dentures. Caulkins played an influential role in Perry's burgeoning artistry. By all accounts innovative, ambitious, and "a keen businessman,"

Caulkins saw the application of his kiln design to china-decorating, ceramics, glass, and enameling. Economic in design, his kiln was versatile and portable. It burned kerosene, an inexpensive and relatively clean fuel, and whether firing for short or long periods, the temperature was constant and could be varied for different parts of the kiln. Caulkins named his invention the Revelation Kiln. Miss Perry marketed the product to china decorators. Her sales approach included demonstrations of various application techniques—enameling, "floating enamels," "raised paste," "dry dusting," and "luster." She helped Caulkins design and publish multiple promotional catalogs under the title *Revelation China & Glass Kilns*, and she traveled throughout the Midwest and larger eastern cities, building the business and making the Revelation Kiln the popular choice for artists and teachers.

Although a successful artist, teacher, and businesswoman, Miss Perry was dissatisfied and restless regarding her future plans. She had offers to head the art department at a girls' school and to work on the staff of a ceramics magazine. While contemplating her future she joined Horace Caulkins' family for a week on Lake Erie at Rondeau Point, Ontario, Canada. It was here that Miss Perry decided to "develop the resources of America." She asked Caulkins if he would help her. He had a full life including family and an established and successful business, yet he sensed her excitement and believed in her talent. He agreed to join her in this undefined artistic effort.

Miss Perry spent countless hours obtaining materials and studying texts on ceramics. She made hundreds of experimental pieces utilizing elements such as cobalt, copper, iron, manganese, nickel, and uranium in different concentrations and temperatures to determine their coloring properties. Here, her father's books proved valuable. She recorded and shared the results of her experiments with Caulkins, who had a fine instinct for chemistry. William Buck Stratton, an architect friend of Miss Perry, taught her about design and form. This early work was done at a carriage house, referred to as "Stable-Studio," on the corner of John R and Alfred Streets in Detroit.

In 1903, having become an expert potter through her unyielding determination, Miss Perry consulted with Burley and Company of Chicago, a leading seller of china and glassware. Mr. Burley gave her an order for one thousand dollars worth of bowls and lamp bases. He also suggested that her product have an identifiable trade name. Previous working names had been "Miss Perry's Pottery" and "Revelation Pottery," named for the kilns used. The Pewabic Mine was located just north of Hancock and the name had persisted in Miss Perry's mind since her childhood days. Pewabic Pottery was born.

The business moved in 1907 to a new Tudor-revival style facility designed by Stratton. This building, at 10125 East Jefferson Avenue in Detroit, was designated a National Historic Landmark in 1991 and remains the home of Pewabic Pottery to this day.

Around this time, Perry, Caulkins, and Stratton helped found the Detroit Society of Arts and Crafts, whose purpose was to promote beautiful objects for everyday use. The Society's first sales room featured the work of local artists, raffia baskets, weavings from the Massachusetts Institute for the Blind, and rocking chairs designed by Labrador fishermen. It was the first and only outlet for handicrafts in Detroit.

"Few people knew or cared about hand-crafted pottery, metal or textiles in those days. The public thought art had to be in a frame or on a pedestal," said Miss Perry.

Driven to explore, Miss Perry's next venture was learning to make tile. This had a practical application as Stratton was designing a home for her on Detroit's East Grand Boulevard. Miss Perry developed tile for the fireplace. Orders for more fireplace tiles soon arrived.

Miss Perry continued her ceramic experiments, varying elements, temperatures, and atmosphere. Her crowning achievement came when her research on oxidizing conditions produced iridescent glazes including the rich red of ancient Persian pottery that some thought not possible. Applying these stunning iridescent glazes to tile moved Pewabic into the larger arena of architecture.

The first major installation of Pewabic tile was the floor of Detroit's Cathedral Church of St. Paul in 1909. This began a tremendous run of installations in churches, businesses, clubs, schools, libraries, private homes, and other structures throughout the greater Detroit area and the country. Many of the leading architects of the day, including Ralph Adams Cram, Cass Gilbert, Bertram Goodhue, Albert Kahn, Charles Maginnis, George D. Mason, Frederick V. Murphy, and Charles Platt included Pewabic tile in their productions.

After working together for many years, Mary Chase Perry and William Buck Stratton were married on June 19, 1918, in the Detroit home of Horace Caulkins. They resided in the home on East Grand Boulevard until 1927. They then took down this home, brick by brick, and incorporated it

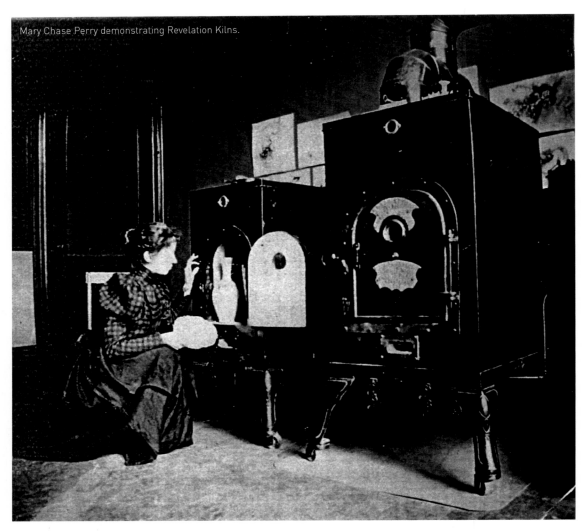

Mary Chase Perry demonstrating Revelation Kilns.

Early example of Pewabic Pottery.

Pewabic House, birthplace of Mary Chase Perry.

Mary Chase Perry Stratton at Pewabic Pottery, Detroit.

Detroit Public Library.

Crypt Church, National Shrine of the Immaculate
Conception, Washington, D.C.

Mary Chase Perry Stratton, one of the most innovative ceramicists in the United States, hails from Hancock.

into a new home, designed by Mr. Stratton and accented with Pewabic tiles throughout, at 938 Three Mile Drive in Grosse Pointe Park, Michigan. This home was listed on the National Register of Historic Places in 1984.

In 1924, Mrs. Stratton received her most notable commission—Pewabic tile for the Crypt Church in the National Shrine of the Immaculate Conception, Washington, D.C. Upon completion of this structure, architect Charles Maginnis stated, "This is one of the most ambitious projects in glazed tile which has ever been undertaken in this country . . . The Stations of the Cross after three years of thought and study represent a fine aesthetic achievement, but they are only a small part of the decorations which Mrs. Stratton has made for the Shrine, all of which are not only beautiful in themselves, but lend themselves perfectly to the architectural demands of the great Crypt of the Shrine."

Another prominent 1920s installation was the Union Trust (now Guardian) Building. Nicknamed the "Cathedral of Finance," this 36-story skyscraper is located in the heart of Detroit's Financial District. Terra cotta Pewabic tiles sheathe the building and Pewabic tile dominates the exterior semi-circular domes and windows. During World War II, the Guardian Building served as the U.S. Army Command Center for wartime production. It was designated a National Historic Landmark in 1989, and it now houses retail shops and offices for Wayne County.

Even today, Most Holy Redeemer Church is the focal point of the West Vernor-Junction Historic District. Located on Detroit's lower west side, adjacent to Mexicantown, Most Holy Redeemer was once the largest Roman Catholic parish in North America and the largest English-speaking parish in the world. This Romanesque church features Pewabic tile murals and lunettes (half-moons). The floors are unglazed terra cotta with glazed ecclesiastical tiles, symbolic of the apostles Matthew (the angel), Mark (the lion), Luke (the ox), and John (the eagle). The floors were installed in 1922 for $12,560.65.

Other historic installations include the Bethel Evangelical Church (now Mayflower Missionary Baptist Church), Detroit; the Detroit Institute of Arts; the Detroit Public Library; the Women's City Club, Detroit; and, buildings at Michigan State University, Oberlin College, Rice University, and the University of Michigan.

Mrs. Stratton remained vital throughout her life. She organized a ceramic department in the University of Michigan's School of Architecture and later received an honorary arts degree from that institution. She received an honorary Ph.D. from Wayne State University for her research in chemicals and glazes. In 1947, she was the recipient of the Charles Fergus Binns Medal, the highest honor bestowed in the field of ceramics in the U.S.

In a talk at the University Club of Detroit, celebrated art collector Charles Lang Freer (1854-1919) stated, "Hundreds of years from now, the names of your motor cars and drug factories may be forgotten, but people will know that Pewabic Pottery was made in Detroit because this beauty will live."

William Buck Stratton died on May 12, 1938. Following his death, Mrs. Stratton donated his architectural portfolio to the Archives of American Art at the Smithsonian. Mary Chase Perry Stratton died on March 16, 1961. She bequeathed her half interest in Pewabic Pottery to Henry L. Caulkins, who had previously received a half interest following the death of his

father Horace. In 1966, ownership of Pewabic Pottery was transferred to Michigan State University, which operated it as a continuing education institution. The Pewabic Society was formed in 1979 to oversee operations, and ownership was transferred to the society in 1981. Today, in addition to designing and fabricating ceramics, Pewabic Pottery features exhibitions, educational programs, and a museum. Recent commercial installations include tile work at Comerica Park, Detroit; the Cranbrook Campus, Bloomfield Hills, Michigan; the Detroit Athletic Club; and, the People Mover, downtown Detroit.

Never accepting an order that did not involve aesthetic adventure, Mary Chase Perry Stratton stated, "It is not the aim of the Pottery to become an enlarged, systematized commercial manufactory in competition with others striving in the same way. Its idea has always been to solve progressively the various ceramic problems that arise in hope of working out the results and artistic effects which may happily remain as memorials . . . or at least stamp this generation as one which brought about a revival of the ceramic arts and prove an inspiration to those who came after us."

Rarely has a vision been so thoroughly realized.

Most Holy Redeemer Church, Detroit. (TOP)
Guardian Building, Detroit. (BOTTOM-LEFT)
Mary Chase Perry Stratton.

Reverend J. K. Nikander

by Karen S. Johnson

Reverend Juho Kustaa Nikander was born in 1855, in Wikkila, Finland, in the parish of Lami, to Johan Kustaa and Hedwig (Metsmaa) Nikander. He was the oldest of three children. His father was a craftsman. While still a boy, Juho decided he would become a minister. He began university studies in Helsinki in 1874, and he completed his theological studies in 1879, graduating with the highest honors. He was ordained in Porvoo the same year.

In January, 1885, Nikander arrived in Hancock to serve congregations there and in Calumet and Allouez, Michigan. He took responsibility for the work started by Reverend A. E. Backman, who served as the region's first Church of Finland pastor.

By 1889, four Church of Finland pastors were serving Finnish-speaking Lutheran congregations in Michigan's Upper Peninsula: J. J. Hoikka, K. L. Tolonen, J. W. Eloheimo, and Nikander. The four pastors met regularly, and in November, 1889, with several others, they began plans for the Finnish Evangelical Lutheran Church of America, also known as the Suomi Synod. In December, 1889, they adopted a constitution and filed articles of incorporation.

On March 25, 1890, at the first meeting of the synod, Nikander was elected president. Early synod districts included Eastern, Ohio-Pennsylvania, Michigan, Minnesota, Columbia, and California. Nikander served as president of the synod from 1890 to 1898 and from 1902 to 1919.

Fearing that many immigrant Finns were in danger of becoming "lost to the church" because there were too few pastors to serve them, the new synod's constitution included a provision to found an *opisto* — an institution of learning — to train pastors and teachers.

The Suomi Synod and its proposed opisto faced both active and passive opposition. Differences in religious outlook, opposition to an educated ministry, and a mistrust of the "Old World" church hierarchy were among the objections.

In September, 1896, the Suomi College and Theological Seminary was opened in rented quarters in Hancock. On May 30, 1899, as many as 2,000 traveled to Hancock for the laying of the cornerstone of the first Suomi College building on Quincy Street, close to the center of town. "Old Main," as the building later came to be called, was dedicated on January 21, 1900. Students and faculty moved from their rented space into their new home that very day.

For eight years, President Nikander resided in Old Main, living and dining with the students. When the college was founded he promised to serve as acting president until a qualified school administrator was hired from Finland. But, when all attempts in that direction failed, the board insisted in 1901 that Nikander consider his call to the presidency his life's work. He fully consented. Pastor and Professor Arnold Stadius wrote that Nikander "was in close contact with every student and he impressed his personality and his thinking upon them all."

Suomi College's golden jubilee publication stated of Nikander, "His quiet persistence in the face of obstacles, his calm conviction, self-effacing devotion to his task, and his vision qualified him for the position of leader of the school. His humble trust in divine guidance and conviction that the call of the college was from God was a source of inspiration and strength to many others." Nikander was 47 years old when he married at the college in the summer of

"His quiet persistence in the face of obstacles, his calm conviction, self-effacing devotion to his task, and his vision qualified him for the position of leader of the school."

1902. He and his wife, Sanna (Rajala), raised three children: Viljo Kustasa, Aino Irene, and Toivo Salomon. They resided at 526 Franklin Street. Nikander was said to have loved children and was a gentle and pious head of the family.

Nikander's own interests were classical languages and Hebrew, which he taught in the seminary, and literary activities. From 1892 until his death, he wrote and published papers for Finnish-American children using the pen name "Juho Setä" (Uncle John). For decades, he edited *Kirkollinen Kalenteri* (the church calendar) and various other college and synod publications.

Nikander was a remarkably active person. Not only was he president of the synod and the college, and a teacher in the seminary, he was a widely published author and editor. He also served as minister to the so-called "Shoreparish," small congregations in the western Upper Peninsula towns of Oskar, Redridge, Elo, Tapiola, Jacobsville, Chassell, Pelkie, Nisula, and Keweenaw Bay.

Before becoming president of the college, Nikander completed numerous mission trips across North America, including to Canada and twice to San Francisco. He traveled to distant and unknown regions, at times having to wade all night through snow. His visits were well-received and he was described as humble and unpretentious.

Nikander served as president of Suomi Synod for 26 years. During his tenure, the number of pastors grew from four to 42 and the number of congregations increased from nine to 155.

Jacob W. Heikkinen wrote that Nikander was "a team person, a true catalyst, a servant pastor, an authentic foreign missionary among his kinsmen in the New World." Raymond W. Wargelin added, "Nikander's personality and integrity created order, established confidence, and won cooperation. Clergy and laymen were drawn to work with him."

In 1896, Nikander, Tolonen, and J. H. Jasberg opened the Finnish Book Store. In 1899, Nikander and several other pastors and laymen formed the Amerikan Suometar Publishing Company and began publishing *The Amerikan Suometar*. Armas K. E. Holmio noted that the newspaper "fostered peaceful national, moral, and religious attitudes in the frequently stormy seas of Finnish-American publishing."

In 1900, *The Amerikan Suometar* and the Finnish Book Store were sold to the Finnish Lutheran Book Concern, which became very important in Finnish-American church life, publishing church literature, Suomi College publications, and other printing.

On January 13, 1919, two days after suffering a stroke, Reverend J. K. Nikander died. He is buried in Hancock's Lakeside Cemetery. Suomi College (now Finlandia University) is his permanent memorial.

Porvoo Cathedral.

Porvoo, Finland
by Mary Pekkala and Glenn Anderson

In July of 1990, the cities of Hancock, Michigan, and Porvoo, Finland, entered into an agreement to begin a sister city relationship under the authority of Sister Cities International. Both cities have since sent numerous delegations on political, economic, and social visits, including a trade mission to Finland in November, 2000, comprised of representatives from Michigan Technological University, Finlandia University, the Keweenaw Industrial Council, and the City of Hancock.

Throughout the years, hockey diplomacy has been a significant part of the unique sister city relationship. The Hancock-Houghton teams and the Porvoo Toldboys teams have visited each other to play in Old Timers hockey tournaments.

Hancock's relationship with Finland has been enhanced over the years with the assistance of Finlandia University. In April, 2000, Prime Minster of Finland Paavo Lipponen visited Hancock to give the commencement address at Finlandia. Tarja Halonen, President of Finland, did the same in April, 2003. During their visits they each attended a program in their honor at Hancock's Barkell Elementary School.

In honor of America's bicentennial in 1976, President of Finland Urho Kekkonen visited the Hancock area and completely filled Michigan Tech's ice arena for his official address to the community. Since 1983, the City of Hancock has had an active Finnish Theme Committee tasked with preserving Finnish heritage locally. The committee continues to thrive and prosper today. Hancock Central High School offers a class where students learn about Finnish language and culture, and the City of Hancock has hosted FinnFest USA multiple times.

Porvoo is Finland's second oldest town and is located about 30 miles east of Helsinki, Finland's capital. A beautiful city full of history, Porvoo has a population of 48,970. The city is bilingual: Finnish is the native language of 65% of the residents, and Swedish is the native language of 32%. Porvoo originally grew as a trade center and it continues to be an attractive focal point of business and commerce.

Settlement in the Porvoo region developed in the 13th and 14th centuries. At the beginning of the 16th century, Danes arrived by sea to destroy the city. The Russians burned Porvoo multiple times, and a fire in 1760 destroyed the majority of the buildings. The present buildings in Old Porvoo were built according to the medieval town plan and are historically significant. Old Porvoo is a popular tourist destination, the parish and church having originated in the 13th century. The Porvoo Cathedral was first built of wood, and later of stone. It sits high on the hill dominating the town. Johan Ludvig Runeberg, the national poet of Finland, lived with his family in Porvoo the last 40 years of his life. He died in Porvoo in 1877, at the age of 73, and his home has been a museum since 1882.

Porvoo, like Hancock, has a proud tradition of supporting the arts. It hosts numerous galleries and artists throughout the city. Both cities continue to support Finnish heritage, culture, international understanding, and fellowship.

John D. Ryan

The Anaconda, an elegantly appointed private car of the Butte, Anaconda, and Pacific Railroad, rolled into Houghton, Michigan's Copper Range Station. It was the 1920s, and John D. Ryan and his wife Nettie were back home to enjoy time with family and friends. In spite of their wealth and prominence, the Ryans were so attached to their memories of the Copper Country and to the values that they absorbed here that they came back for regular visits. They even insisted that their only son, John Carlos, enroll at the Michigan College of Mines (now Michigan Technological University) to experience something of the culture and community that meant so much to them. Even the detractors of this "Montana Copper King," a master planner and manager of technological progress, corporate consolidations, and free-wheeling financial manipulations, acknowledged his down-home values and his total lack of the pomp and flamboyance that were so common among the business elite of his time.

HANCOCK 1863 - 2013

by Corbin Eddy

John D. Ryan was baptized Johannes Dionysius on October 12, 1864, in St. Anne's Church, a simple wood-frame structure at the corner of Ravine and Quincy Streets. He was born in Pewabic just two days earlier to Irish immigrant parents John C. and Johanna O'Donnell Ryan. Father Edward Jacker, the pioneer founder of the Catholic Church in Hancock, administered the sacrament.

John C. Ryan and his brothers, William and Edward, immigrated to the United States 20 years earlier from Limerick Junction, County Tipperary, Munster, Ireland. The local lead and copper mines were beginning to flounder and the Ryan brothers sought new opportunities. They were fortunate enough to have sufficient resources to come to America together and were able to move quickly away from the immigrant ghettos of east coast cities.

Initially they settled in Wiota, Lafayette County, the lead-mining district of Wisconsin, where John C. tried his hand at farming. By 1854, all three brothers had relocated to Michigan's Copper Country.

The Ryans were not part of the massive number of Irish emigrants triggered by the Great Famine, but they were deeply influenced by them. They settled in, married, and made their home among them, quickly becoming their leaders and advocates in a new world.

John C. Ryan and Johanna O'Donnell, an Irish immigrant and a "refugee" of the potato famine, were married in 1854. They raised three daughters and two sons. Both John C. and his brother William were deeply involved in the initial exploratory stages and as captains and superintendents of copper mines that subsequently opened

in the area. They were both strong and capable managers of mining interests as well as effective leaders of the labor force.

Both of John D.'s parents fully expected him to pursue higher education, perhaps in engineering, and to follow his father into the local mining industry. Never having been very interested in school and admitting that he was "not much of a student," he set out instead to earn some money and establish his independence.

As destiny would have it, and though later admitting that he "never did a day's work in the mines," the copper-mining industry was looming in John D.'s future. At 17 years of age, he went to work for his uncle, Edward, the "Merchant Prince of the Copper Country." For eight years he worked out of the Ryan General Store at 125-127 Quincy Street. His relationship with his uncle and what he learned from him and from his customers were formative of his developing skills and personality.

Although he had never pictured himself an entrepreneur, a banker, or community leader, John D. picked up from his uncle and from his experience in his uncle's business what would later be called "incredible horse sense:" a strong and practical business head, a savvy way of dealing with the public, and a sense of responsibility to the broader community.

In 1889, four years after his father's death, John D. decided to move on from the Copper Country. His brother William and sister Julia, both in poor health, had already left Hancock and moved to Denver, Colorado. John D. joined them there, scarcely imagining that the next major stop on his journey would be Butte, Montana, the heart of another copper country. His sister Alice, then Sr. Agnes Gonzaga, C.S.J., joined them in Denver from 1893 to 1896.

Not ready to rush into anything, John D. looked around for six months before he accepted a full-time job. He was hired as a salesman for the Crew-Levick Oil Company, traveling from Montana to the Mexican border selling lubricating oil to companies and institutions large and small. Building on his retail experience, his time as a traveling salesman along with his keen intellect and curiosity taught him how companies and organizations were put together. From a discreet distance, he gained insight into how the imagination, ingenuity, and negotiating skills of strong leaders made organizations successful, and ultimately profitable. The stage was being set for him to become a major social and economic player himself, embracing the challenges, opportunities, and temptations inherent in the American capitalist system of the time.

A key personality and mentor whom Ryan met in his travels would become another major influence in his developing personal and professional career. Marcus Daly was the founder and president of the Anaconda Copper Mining Company. Himself an Irish immigrant, Daly was intelligent, ambitious and industrious. After purchasing a small silver deposit called the Anaconda, he discovered that it contained a huge body of copper. He entered into partnership with three others who provided the capital for him to develop what would evolve into a huge enterprise. His partners were less enthusiastic, speculating that the market for copper was quite limited, far to the east, and already monopolized by Michigan's Copper Country. Anticipating great expansion in the market, Daly gambled that with large-scale production he could compete with anyone. The rapid growth of Anaconda attests to his solid instincts. By 1887, the Montana mines became the leading copper-producing region in the nation, ahead of Michigan and Arizona.

After several expansions and reorganizations, Standard Oil partners Henry H. Rogers and William Rockefeller purchased Anaconda, created the Amalgamated Copper Mining Company, and appointed Daly as president.

As western regional manager for Crew-Levick, Ryan had an important client in Daly. The two formed a close friendship, Daly appreciating Ryan's quick mind and charm, and Ryan appreciating Daly's gentlemanly counsel. Ryan was introduced to Amalgamated's corporate lawyer, Cornelius "Con" Kelley, who would become a lifelong colleague and friend.

In 1896, John D.'s proposal of marriage to Nettie Gardner would profoundly change his life. At 32 years old, he was earning $200 a month as a traveling salesman and sharing a home and office with his brother William, an arrangement that was quite satisfactory until Nettie became central to the picture. She was a sophisticated, attractive, artistic, and musical woman from a prominent family back in Houghton with which his uncle Edward had long business and personal associations.

Nettie's mother, Sarah Wales Dashiell, was valedictorian of her class at St. Mary's in Poughkeepsie, New York, and she shared the stage with General Ulysses S. Grant, who gave the commencement address. The general was very impressed with her speech and her poise. He commented to her that he would be anxious to know how her life would develop and invited her to keep in touch with him. She subsequently married Grenville Gardner and had two daughters. Gardner's drinking habits, however, became so intolerable that she divorced him and insisted that he have no further contact with her or their daughters. Struggling with the responsibilities of a single mother, she "swallowed hard"

and contacted then President Grant. He did remember her and arranged for her to have a job in the Library of Congress.

It was there that Sarah met her future husband, Carlos Shelden. The son of Random Shelden, Edward Ryan's first boss and mentor, Carlos served throughout the U.S. Civil War as captain in the 23rd Regiment, Michigan Volunteer Infantry. At the end of his service he returned to Houghton County and engaged in mining, machining, real estate, and the steamboat business. He was later elected to serve in both the Michigan House of Representatives and Senate before being elected in 1896 for the first of three terms in the U.S. Congress from Michigan's 12th District.

"The marriage of Miss Nettie Gardner of Houghton to John D. Ryan, formerly of Hancock, now of Denver, Colorado, was solemnized Wednesday of last week, November 12, 1896, by Rev. Father Atfield, pastor of St. Patrick's Church, at the home of the bride's parents, newly elected Congressman and Mrs. Carlos D. Shelden. It was a glittering social event. The couple will make their home in Denver." So reported the media of the day.

John D.'s brother William, never in robust health, died in Denver shortly after the wedding. Using his inheritance from William, his own savings, and all that he could borrow, John D. began his business pursuits by buying up stocks in the Daly Bank and Trust Company until he became an important stockholder. He then moved with his wife to Butte. It was there that his relationship with Marcus Daly and his family solidified. By the time Daly died in November, 1900, John D. had his complete confidence and that of his widow, Margaret Daly. He was named president of Daly Bank and Trust and trustee of Margaret's inherited assets.

As Amalgamated Copper Mining Company's banker, he quickly came to the attention of John D. Rockefeller's most aggressive partner, Henry H. Rogers, who appointed him managing director with entire charge of all its subsidiaries. His responsibilities extended not only to the management of the company's assets and properties, but to its personnel and labor force. With virtually no formal education or managerial experience, the challenges Ryan faced could not have been more complex.

Marcus Daly had personally been at the heart of Anaconda's development and was highly respected throughout Montana, but with him gone the company was now in the control of "oily Easterners" who were resented by miners and managers alike. Amalgamated had fierce legal and political battles on its hands and labor conditions were unsettled, even violent. The company was neck deep in litigation with Fritz Augustus Heinze, another man who would be crucial in Ryan's development as a person and businessman, this time not an uncle, a friend, or a mentor, but a formidable adversary.

The background, experience, and temperament of Heinze could not have been more different from that of Ryan. Heinze located, purchased, and developed one of Butte's most ore-rich properties, but felt that he had to "catch up" as he arrived in the area well after the other "Copper Kings," including Daly, were established. One of his strategies was to reduce the working day for his miners from ten to eight hours. It was a cynical move designed to destabilize the labor force employed by his much larger competitors. Another strategy was to mine veins that outcropped from his claim, even beneath claims owned by others. Known as the "law of apex," its legality was being challenged in court. This

didn't stop Heinze from moving deep into Amalgamated property to extract a hundred thousand tons of high-grade copper ore. There was much violence between the miners of the two companies, including hand-to-hand combat, and Heinze eventually caved in the property with dynamite to obliterate the evidence of his activities.

Heinze used his influence to ensure that "friendly" people, including judges, were appointed to important positions in Montana. He became a brilliant orator, and in political speeches he painted the Amalgamated Company and its management as ruthless and oppressive. He took full advantage of the "oily Easterners" characterization of Rockefeller and Rogers, and he told the miners that Amalgamated "will force you to dwell in Standard Oil houses while you live, and be buried in Standard Oil coffins when you die."

In 1906, after a decade of the mining war, and after most of Heinze's political collaborators were defeated in the election, Ryan sensed an opening for negotiations. Ryan wished to remove Heinze "root and branch" from the scene, but knew that his fiercely-proud adversary could not "lose face." Any deal would have to appear to be a merger.

Mortally afraid that the miners would learn that he was preparing to sell out at the same time as he was flamboyantly promising to fight their battles, Heinze would only meet Ryan in secret, arriving at agreed-upon locations at different times and entering through different doors. They finally reached a deal at three in the morning in a Providence, Rhode Island, hotel. Heinze accepted 12 million dollars and quietly left the mining world. Meanwhile, Rogers and the Rockefeller investors gradually became majority shareholders in Montana's United Copper

Company to create a near-monopoly in the global copper market. By 1910, Amalgamated had bought out several other smaller companies and controlled virtually all of the copper-mining operations in the state.

Ryan took pride in the fact that after Heinze's disappearance he was able to manage threats of labor difficulties. He made it clear to all that good wages would be paid and that good service was expected. Remembering the much smaller mining operations that had been in the charge of his father and his uncle William, he made it his business to visit the properties personally to socialize with the miners and to insist that they come to him if they had a grievance. They got used to calling him "John" and always got a hearing, although from time to time he had to tell them to "go to hell" if he judged that their complaints had no merit. There were, however, serious and even violent labor disturbances on the horizon, but they arose from the struggle of two larger unions[1] to gain control of the Butte Miners' Union. Ryan took the daring independent decision to stick with his personal and paternalistic negotiating strategies. He refused to recognize either faction, and declared an "open shop" in all the company's properties.

Ryan's management acumen so impressed Rogers, whose health by now was failing, that he called him to New York to prepare him for larger responsibilities. After Rogers' death in 1908, Ryan was named president of an expanded Amalgamated. Commonly known in Montana simply as "the Company," the operations were officially renamed Anaconda. It was a way to create a new company after the Heinze "merger," and a way for Ryan to honor the memory of Marcus Daly, the friend and mentor who inspired his first days in the industry. Although he continued to consider Montana his home, Ryan bought Rogers'

five-story, neo-French Renaissance town house at 3 E 78th Street, just off of upper 5th Avenue, in Manhattan, New York, and settled there with his wife and only son, John Carlos, as he steadily evolved into a national industrial giant.

Ahead of his time, the creative and visionary Ryan was ready to undertake another project. He had long considered the potential for hydro-electric power in Montana and was dreaming of ways to develop it. Available coal was of poor quality and had to be transported great distances by trains, which themselves burned coal along the way to power their steam engines. In powering mining operations, coal was not only expensive, but "dirty and dangerous." Its smoke and fumes were toxic.

The Missouri River and its Montana tributaries fall 10,000 feet between the divide of the watersheds and the eastern border of the state. Practically limitless power could potentially be generated and made available through the state. Two groups of small, local power plants existed at the time, one in Butte and one in Great Falls. Ryan set about not only to finance their purchase and consolidate them, but to provide linkage in between the two cities with transmission lines, sub-stations, and new storage dams. By 1910, he had developed the great Rainbow Dam that would supply 15,000 horsepower of electricity to the Butte mines, and by 1913, the Butte, Anaconda, and Pacific Railroad was completely electrified between the mines in Butte and the smelters in and around Anaconda, Montana.

The Montana Power Company, which Ryan founded and led, furnished not only the power necessary to operate the mines, but virtually all of the electricity for industrial, commercial, and domestic use in Montana. Anti-trust politicians

Reverend Edward Jacker
by Corbin Eddy

Born in Ellwangen, Württemberg, Germany, on September 2, 1827, Edward Jacker was the private tutor for a wealthy family when he felt the call to religious life and came to the United States in 1854. He joined the German Benedictine Foundation at Latrobe, Pennsylvania. Now St. Vincent Archabbey, it remains a flourishing community with a college and a seminary.

Fascinated by tales of Native American missionaries, Jacker received permission to leave the Benedictine community. He applied to and was accepted by Bishop Baraga, then Vicar Apostolic of Upper Michigan, and he was ordained to the priesthood on August 5, 1855, in Sault Ste. Marie. This was the second ordination for what became the Diocese of Marquette.

Father Jacker was sent to L'Anse/Assinins, where he set himself to a study of the language and culture of the local tribe as well as to the service of the European settlers. In 1860, he received the additional responsibility of St. Ignatius Church in Houghton, to which he walked every other week. Hancock was soon added to his responsibilities.

Father Jacker resigned his pastorate of L'Anse/ Assinins in 1861, and he set himself to founding and building St. Anne's Parish in Hancock, where he chose to make his home. The church was dedicated on August 4, 1861. Always something of a monk at heart, Father Jacker gathered a community of students around him. This included William Dwyer, a young man who would later serve as a pastor.

In 1866, when Bishop Baraga went to Baltimore, Maryland, for the Second Plenary Council of Bishops, Father Jacker was named administrator of the diocese in Marquette. The bishop returned an invalid, and Father Jacker continued to administer the diocese after Baraga's death until the appointment of Ignatius Mrak as his successor.

Instead of returning to Hancock and expanding his student community, Father Jacker went to Calumet, to organize Sacred Heart Parish. He subsequently served as diocesan administrator once again when Bishop Mrak traveled to Rome, Italy, for the First Vatican Council in 1873. After that, Father Jacker was assigned to St. Ignace, where, along with his pastoral duties, he undertook extensive historical and archeological studies of early mission foundations, including the identification and restoration of Father Marquette's grave site, which had been forgotten for centuries.

When Bishop Mrak resigned in 1878, Father Jacker once again became diocesan administrator. He returned to his beloved Hancock after Bishop Vertin took office in 1879. He considered the St. Anne's reorganization, later to become two parishes (St. Patrick's and St. Joseph's), to be a project beyond his strength at that time, and in 1884, he instead chose to retire to Eagle Harbor, for study and prayer. Even there his pastoral duties turned out to be more than he felt he could handle. After going downstate to Detour, Michigan, and suffering through an exceptionally severe winter, Reverend Edward Jacker died in Marquette on September 1, 1887. His body was returned to Hancock, where his funeral was held. He is buried in the Catholic cemetery which is now the site of Church of the Resurrection. A memorial monument to the pioneer priest of the community greets visitors at the church entrance.

[Eds. note: All of the municipalities mentioned herein are in Michigan's Upper Peninsula unless noted otherwise.]

had Ryan called before a congressional committee in Washington, D.C., on the charge that he had created and controlled a state monopoly. He stunned the committee by affirming that his company, now commonly called "the Power," was a de facto monopoly because the service was so good and the cost so low that no one could even consider going into competition with him. The committee's subsequent research proved him correct and revealed that Montana led the world in per capita consumption of clean electric energy.

When World War I broke out, Ryan made the surprising decision to resign his position as president of Anaconda and offer his service to the Red Cross. He was appointed director of military relief, a position that offered scope for his organizational skills to make a constructive contribution to the war effort.

The "right hand" of John D. Ryan was Cornelius Kelley, whom he had met as a young lawyer who was also being mentored by Marcus Daly. Ryan had such confidence in Kelley, then serving as vice president, that he turned the presidency over to him.

Ryan's work with the Red Cross brought him to the attention of President Woodrow Wilson, who in the spring of 1918 appointed him second assistant secretary of war. In that capacity Ryan served as director of aircraft production for the Army. He was charged with organizing and supervising the production of military aircraft, an area that had been incompetently managed. Airplane engines, for example, were being ordered in large quantity and it was not until months had been spent on their manufacture that it was discovered that they were far too large to be practical in the type of plane that would be effective against German forces.

Ryan was an unlikely but bold choice for such a position. He was not an engineer, and knew nothing about airplanes. He reportedly began his service by blocking out six weeks to study the situation during which time he would refuse all calls and interviews. It was, however, within nine days that he was called to make a report on his progress. He had already identified the type of plane that would best fulfill the Army's stated needs, and he had made major progress in solving the internal communication and management problems of the department. He was subsequently able to lay the groundwork for large scale production of aircraft, but the war ended before many of the planes were in service.

When he returned to Anaconda after the war, Ryan did not reassume the presidency but served as chairman of the board. He and Kelley formed a team that led Anaconda through its golden years. The copper-mining industry had lurched from wartime peak production to postwar surpluses. In 1921, most American copper mines had completely shut down. The price of copper quickly rebounded and mining activity increased. Managed by a dexterous Ryan-Kelley team, "the Company" was growing and expanding into new areas of activity: manganese, zinc, aluminum, uranium, and silver.

In 1922, Anaconda purchased its best customer, American Brass Company, the nation's largest brass fabricator and a major consumer of copper and zinc. Unable to supply its demands, Ryan and Kelley sought and gained control of mining operations in Chile and Mexico. The Chuquicamata in Chile was the largest copper mine in the world with the lowest operating cost. It quickly became the source of two-thirds to three-fourths of Anaconda's profits. The importance of the Butte mines was diminishing, but the high profits from Chile were able to balance out Montana's higher cost, labor-intensive mines at the same time giving Kelley and Ryan clout over any threat of increased taxes or labor demands. In 1926, the company acquired the Giesch Corporation, a large mining and industrial firm operating in the Upper Silesia region of Poland. By that time Anaconda had become the fourth-largest company in the world.

As he reached 60, Ryan seemed to be mellowing. He had always protected his privacy and avoided the spotlight, but his personal privacy became almost an obsession. He insisted on confidentiality and anonymity for his extensive philanthropic activities. He appeared most at ease in his own home and during family vacations in Michigan's Copper Country, where he felt that he could be "himself."

In 1928, however, Ryan and Percy Rockefeller aggressively got into a "pump and dump" speculating routine with Anaconda stock. This practice, both legal and quite common in its day, had them buying up thousands of shares causing their value to rise, then selling them off, causing their value to fall, and then buying them back. They had a joint account with close to one and a half million shares. They were also trading in securities of other international copper companies such as the Chile Copper Company, Greene Cananea Copper Company, and the Andes Copper Mining Company, all of which were acquired by Anaconda. These stocks, called "the coppers," were among the hottest speculative items on the market. When the stock market ultimately crashed in October, 1929, the price of copper dropped dramatically, and Anaconda suffered a setback from which it took years to recover.

After the crash and during the depression, the U.S. Senate Committee on Banking and Currency conducted hearings on stock exchange practices. In his June 4, 1932 testimony, Ryan acknowledged that their speculative practices and market maneuvers had been lucrative for those who cashed out, but that he personally had suffered a "very serious loss" by holding on to his own Anaconda stock while its price sank from $175 to $4 per share. To their credit, as the depression deepened, Ryan and Kelley, mindful of their responsibilities to miners and their families, kept the now unprofitable Butte mines open and functioning.

On Friday, February 10, 1933, Ryan suffered a heart attack after morning mass at St. Ignatius Loyola Church on Park Avenue in New York, which he attended on an almost daily basis. Two physicians were attending to him at his home when he died the next morning. His remains were borne in a copper casket into a packed St. Ignatius Church the following Tuesday morning where a solemn funeral mass was celebrated.

At the time of his death, Ryan was under subpoena to appear once again before the Senate subcommittee regarding stock market practices. Ferdinand Pecora, counsel for the subcommittee, commented publicly that unlike many of his colleagues, Ryan "placed at the disposal of the committee promptly and willingly all information requested of him and manifested throughout a desire to cooperate." The conclusion of the committee, however, was that the stock manipulation of "the coppers" was one of the greatest frauds in American banking history and a major cause of the depression.

In the years that followed, Ryan's friend and colleague Con Kelley became known as "Mr. Anaconda," guiding "the Company" through trying times of operating losses. When the Great Depression ended, Anaconda was debt-free and ready to begin again. "The Company" was purchased by Atlantic Richfield Company (ARCO) in 1977. ARCO became a subsidiary of British Petroleum (BP) in 2000.

Nettie Gardner Ryan stayed on at their Manhattan home from which she quietly oversaw the family's charitable interests and raised funds for various organizations assisting needy children.

[1] This included the Western Federation of Miners and its president, Charles H. Moyer, who was unceremoniously deported from the Copper Country in 1913 after being shot in Hancock's Scott Hotel. Moyer fared no better in butting heads with Ryan. Following a good deal of violence, Moyer was run out of Butte in 1914.

Ryan Hall, Fontbonne University, St. Louis. (TOP)

Ryan home, 3 E 78th Street, Manhattan.

...a strong and practical business head, a savvy way of dealing with the public, and a sense of responsibility to the broader community.

John D. Ryan.

Sister Jean Frances Haug, 1959.

St. Joseph's Hospital, 1904 building, later named Ryan Hall.

St. Joseph's Hospital
by Corbin Eddy

In 1899, Frederick Eis, Bishop of Marquette, learned that the Sisters of St. Francis would be withdrawing from St. Mary's Hospital in Hancock, which they had founded just three years earlier in Bishop John Vertin's family home. The bishop contacted the mother superior of the Sisters of St. Joseph of Carondelet in St. Louis, Missouri, with the hope that they would be able to take over a clearly difficult challenge in the "far north." As providence had it, there were nursing sisters who had just arrived back in New York after serving in Cuba during the Spanish American War. They were sent to a very different "island," the Keweenaw Peninsula.

As the public and local physicians gained confidence in the sisters, the hospital outgrew the Vertin house and a new St. Joseph's Hospital on Water Street was dedicated in 1904. The building was unique to the area, designed in the style of a Renaissance chateau appropriate to the French roots of the Sisters of St. Joseph. Perched high above the canal, it featured formal entrances, ornate masonry, turrets, and gables. Its interior had paneled ceilings and carefully detailed oak window and door frames.

Another war veteran, this time of World War I, Sister Irmina Dougherty was sent to Hancock in 1920 to organize a school of nursing, which was accredited by the Michigan Board of Nursing in 1923. As the school and community continued to grow, a chapel was added to the hospital and a nurses' residence was constructed in 1929 with funds donated by John D. Ryan.

A new, nine-story hospital was constructed in 1951, providing for the care and service of 125 patients. An important feature of the new hospital was its capacity to house long-term geriatric patients, a growing need in the community. With the completion of the new building the entire old hospital was refurbished for the school of nursing and it was renamed Ryan Hall. The nurses' residence became the convent for the sisters.

Sister John Kenneth Scott was named directress of St. Joseph's School of Nursing in 1965. A strong advocate for community nursing education, she oversaw the program until its last commencement in 1974. At that time, she and her religious community were confident that nursing education would continue in the Copper Country at Finlandia University and Michigan Technological Univeristy[1].

The transition from sponsorship of the hospital by the sisters to a nonprofit corporation had already begun under the direction of Sister Jean Frances Haug and was completed in 1976. The hospital, now completely under the direction of a board of lay trustees and administered by a contract management team based in Tennessee, was renamed Portage View Hospital.

In the ensuing years, the 1929 nurses' residence that had become a convent was remodeled once again for medical offices. With the school of nursing closed, Ryan Hall stood empty, and by 1985, it had deteriorated to such a point that the hospital board voted to demolish the structure for reasons of public safety.

Portage View Hospital became Portage Health in 1995, and a completely new campus was opened on Quincy Hill in 2000. The 1951 hospital and the 1929 nurses' residence now comprise Finlandia University's Jutila Center.

[1] Finlandia continues to offer degrees in nursing through its College of Health Science. The Michigan Tech Senate voted in 1980 to terminate its nursing program.

It was clear to her from the outset of her leadership that the 20th century was calling for new methods of teaching, nursing, and child care, and that the education and training of the sisters would need to keep up with these developments.

Reverend Mother Agnes Gonzaga Ryan, C.S.J.[1]

by Corbin Eddy

Alice Ryan was born January 22, 1855, the eldest child of John C. and Johanna O'Donnell Ryan. As a Catholic parish had not yet been founded in Hancock, she was baptized at St. Ignatius in Houghton, Michigan, by Bishop Frederic Baraga during one of his regular visits to the area. Strong, lifelong Catholics, the Ryans were welcoming and supportive of the Sisters of St. Joseph of Carondelet, who came to Hancock from St. Louis, Missouri, in 1866, to found St. Anne's School.

Following her education at St. Anne's, Alice felt called to become a sister herself. For such a gifted and highly motivated young woman, life as a Sister of St. Joseph would offer an orderly and disciplined approach to her personal and spiritual growth. It would likewise offer a path to professional development and service in the world. Both were high priorities for her and she was ready and eager to answer the call to this life of dedicated service. In a highly patriarchal world, communities of religious women were making remarkable contributions, to the church and to society at large, that would lie well beyond the capacity of individuals or even of less formally organized groups. She entered the Troy (New York) Province of the Sisters of St. Joseph in 1873 and made her final profession as Sister Agnes Gonzaga on March 19, 1876.

From 1876 to 1887, she taught in Troy and Glens Falls, New York, before being assigned to Albany, New York, where she was appointed superintendent of schools for her order. At 30 years of age she was already superior[2] of a convent in Glens Falls. When her father died in 1885, the difficulties of long distance travel and the discipline of her order made it impossible for her to be at his bedside, but she wired him the following message: "I cannot

come. Goodbye, father. Thank you. I'll meet you in heaven." John C. was buried in Hancock's Catholic cemetery, now the site of Church of the Resurrection.

Sister Agnes Gonzaga joined her siblings in Denver, Colorado, in 1893, where she served as a school principal. Then, in 1896, she was elected to the General Council of her order and moved to the motherhouse in the St. Louis neighborhood of Carondelet. In 1905, she was elected superior general[3] of the congregation, which now spread from New York to California and from the Great Lakes to the Gulf of Mexico.

It was clear to her from the outset of her leadership that the 20th century was calling for new methods of teaching, nursing, and child care, and that the education and training of the sisters would need to keep up with these developments. She saw to it that salaries for the sisters in their various missions were raised both to improve their living conditions as well as to fund the education of their members in colleges and universities around the world.

Reverend Mother traveled to Rome, Italy, in December, 1908. She and her party had a private audience with Pope Pius X in early January. Later in the month she was present in the consistory of the Vatican for the pronouncement of the beatification of Joan of Arc.

Upon her return to St. Louis, she supervised the plans for a new St. Joseph's Hospital in Kansas City, Missouri, and she attended its ground-breaking in 1915. Having previously served as directress of St. Joseph's Academy, a preparatory high school for girls attached to the motherhouse, she dreamt of her order sponsoring a college for young women. She initiated the purchase of land in St. Louis where

Fontbonne University now stands. The school's charter was approved on April 17, 1917.

Suffering physically and knowing her death was approaching, Reverend Mother Agnes Gonzaga Ryan tendered her resignation that May. She died on June 14, 1917.

World War I delayed Fontbonne's construction and the initial classes were held at St. Joseph's Academy in 1923. Ground was broken in 1924 for the first of five projected buildings in the college's long-range plan. Alice's brother, John D. Ryan, quietly contributed funds so that all five buildings could be completed at the same time. Classes began on the new campus in 1925 and the five buildings were completed and dedicated the following year. John D. traveled from New York and his sister Margaret Gaul from Houghton to attend the dedication. The administration building was to be named for him in tribute to his generosity. He insisted instead that the name honor his sister, whose dream for the continuing education of young women had been realized.

Fontbonne University evolved into a coeducational institution, admitting males to all degree programs in 1974. Ryan Hall stands majestically in the center of campus to this day.

[1] C.S.J. refers to the Congregation (Sisters) of St. Joseph.

[2] This position bestowed upon her the title of Mother.

[3] This position bestowed upon her the title of Reverend Mother.

Ryan Hall, Fontbonne University, St. Louis.

HANCOCK 1863 - 2013

Dr. Joseph E. Scallon

by Marty Schendel

On February 25, 1853, six years prior to the Quincy Mining Company's platting of the land that became Hancock, a future leading citizen of Hancock and prominent figure in the medical community was born in Brooklyn, New York. The child was Joseph Edward Scallon.

Joseph's father, who emigrated from Ireland in 1810, moved his family from Brooklyn to Joliette, Quebec, Canada, to pursue employment in the lumber industry. Joseph received a classical education there.

In 1870, Joseph joined the Papal Zouaves, a volunteer military unit formed to protect the Papal States. His contingent headed for Italy to assist Pope Pius IX. They made it as far as France before turning back upon receiving news of the capture of Rome on September 20, 1870.

After returning to Quebec, Joseph entered Laval University in Quebec City, where he studied medicine for two years. He next attended Victoria College of Medicine and Surgery at Montreal, from which he graduated in 1874.

The young Dr. Scallon began his practice in Negaunee, Michigan, serving the medical needs of the mining and logging community and making the Upper Peninsula his home. Times were tough and securing enough patients to make a living was difficult. Dr. Scallon developed a plan by which French lumberjacks and others who were without the services of a mining company doctor could pay a monthly fee of $0.50 to retain the services of their own private physician — a 19th-century HMO! Unfortunately, the majority of the mines soon closed and with them went Dr. Scallon's clientele. A smallpox epidemic then broke out in Negaunee and the village employed Dr. Scallon to manage the pest house (an infirmary for communicable diseases). For this he was paid $150.00, considerably more than he had managed since arriving in the Upper Peninsula.

After a year in Negaunee, Dr. Scallon made his next and final move, to Hancock. Almost immediately he began serving the community as both a physician and public figure. In March, 1876, he spoke at a meeting of the Emerald Literary Society and helped raise funds to establish a library at St. Patrick's Hall. Dr. Scallon was village president from 1891 to 1893 and he was involved in establishing Hancock's water and sewer systems. He served on the local school board for 22 years and he was instrumental in the founding of the county sanitarium. Dr. Scallon held multiple positions as a public health official including county superintendent of the poor. He was very active in Catholic organizations, serving the Ancient Order of Hibernians at the state and national level and organizing a local chapter of the Catholic Men's Benevolent Association. Dr. Scallon also chaired the Democratic congressional and county committees and he was a member of the Ancient Order of United Workmen.

In the medical profession, Dr. Scallon was described as being "in the front ranks." He was a fellow in the American College of Surgeons and dean of the staff at Hancock's St. Joseph's Hospital. Druggist George H. Nichols said of Dr. Scallon, "His entire life was devoted to the advancement of others. As a physician he did his work conscientiously and without regard for his own welfare and as a public official his honesty and integrity were never questioned."

"His entire life was devoted to the advancement of others. As a physician he did his work conscientiously and without regard for his own welfare and as a public official his honesty and integrity were never questioned."

Dr. Scallon was fluent in French and when famed actress Sarah Bernhardt visited the Copper Country, Dr. Scallon served as both her escort and interpreter.

Dr. Scallon married Bridget Agnes Finnegan, of Houghton, Michigan, on October 1, 1877. Her father, Michael Finnegan, was previously sheriff of Houghton County, and her brother, Jeremiah T. Finnegan, was later a prominent local attorney who handled the legal work of incorporating Hancock as a city in March, 1903.

The Scallons lived in the 300 block of Hancock Street. In 1904, they purchased lots 31 and 32 in Block 11 of Condon's Third Addition to Hancock, later addressed 1209 W. Quincy Street. On this hillside property with a view of Portage Lake, Dr. Scallon built a magnificent structure which served as his home and office.

Five of the Scallon's children survived into adulthood: Margaret, Mary, Edward Philip, Ann, and Brighidin. Mrs. Scallon died in 1907. In the fall of 1924, Dr. Scallon traveled to Helena, Montana, to visit his brother William, who was a prominent western attorney. William Scallon had previously served as president of the Amalgamated (Anaconda) Copper Mining Company, succeeding Marcus Daly and preceding John D. Ryan. Following several weeks with his brother, Dr. Scallon traveled to Crosby, Minnesota, to visit his son. Edward Philip Scallon was serving his first of six consecutive terms in the Minnesota House of Representatives at the time. Dr. Scallon died of cancer while in Crosby, on November 9, 1924. With the exception of Brighidin who was studying in Paris, France, at the time, all of his children were at his bedside. Dr. Scallon's body was returned to Hancock, and he is buried in the Catholic cemetery that is now the site of Church of the Resurrection. Former Hancock mayor Thomas Coughlin stated, "In the life of Dr. Scallon we shall see much to admire. He cared but little for wealth and was always true to his friends. He has left a heritage which riches cannot buy." Scallon Street is named in his honor.

Sarah Bernhardt.

Phi Kappa Tau
by Marty Schendel

Following the death of Dr. Joseph E. Scallon in 1924, his home at 1209 W. Quincy Street went vacant and remained so for many years. In 1945, Ray and Margaret Hill purchased the home and operated it as a boarding house known as the Ray Hill Hotel. The Hills sold the property in 1954 to Thomas and Helen Smith, who occupied it for a brief time. The home sat vacant again for almost three years and was referred to as the "old ghost house" on Quincy Street.

Meanwhile, on April 2, 1957, a new college fraternity was formed by twelve students, mostly freshmen, who were interested in an organization open to all men of the Michigan College of Mining and Technology (now Michigan Technological University) regardless of race, color, religion, or economic status. This group of students and their advisor, Humanities Professor Joe Kirkish, founded Mu Kappa Mu (MKM), a social fraternity.

Membership in MKM quickly swelled to over 30, and a housing committee was charged with locating a property that the fraternity could call home. After turning down several opportunities in Houghton, home to Tech and the location preferred by school officials, the group settled on the old Ray Hill Hotel in Hancock.

Life was once again breathed into 1209 West Quincy in the fall of 1957, following a deal brokered by prominent local businessman Ted Reiss between the Smiths and this band of fraternity brothers from Michigan Tech. With the assistance of Superior National Bank and Trust, the property changed hands on September 1, 1957. Over the next five years, ten more lots, both on the north and south side of Quincy Street, were added to the parcel owned by the fraternity.

Life was not easy for the men of MKM that first year. In addition to keeping up with the rigors of school, they had to make their monthly payment to the bank; purchase furniture, beds, and desks for the house; and, keep the pantry stocked for their new fraternity cook, Laura Archambeau. The members decided that they needed the benefits provided by affiliating with a national fraternity, and they selected Phi Kappa Tau (ΦKT), based in Oxford, Ohio.

Soon after being accepted as the Gamma Alpha chapter of ΦKT, the men of 1209 West Quincy were recognized at the national level for their leadership, scholarship, motivation, philanthropy, and community involvement. Awards were regularly shipped north from Oxford as few of the national executives were willing to drive to Hancock, which they considered to be just south of the Arctic Circle!

Activities that the fraternity participates in today include Michigan Tech's annual Winter Carnival, the Michigan Department of Transportation's Adopt-A-Highway program, the Hancock Public Schools' pancake breakfast, the Kiwanis Club of the Copper Country's chicken barbeque, building ramps for the handicapped, Christmas caroling, tutoring, fundraising for local organizations, raking leaves for the elderly, and much more.

Dr. Scallon would be proud that his property overlooking the lake remains an integral part of the community and that its MKM inhabitants have made a visible and lasting impact on the Tech campus, the city of Hancock, and the surrounding area for over 55 years.

Her lifetime was witness to 29 U.S. presidents, the U.S. Civil War, World Wars I and II, and immeasurable social and technological changes.

HANCOCK 1863 - 2013

Mamie Nelson

by John S. Haeussler

What common trait do U.S. Presidents James Monroe and Harry S. Truman share? They both resided in the White House during Mamie Nelson's lifetime, which spanned over 123 years!

Mamie was born in County Cork, Ireland, on February 3, 1825. King George IV reigned at that time, his father having been the monarch who lost the American colonies in the Revolutionary War. Mamie's father was a saltwater captain who sailed from the Spanish Main to the Western Pacific Ocean. She spent her youth aboard brigantines and sloops with her father, carrying cargo to Australia, China, Japan, India, America, and other locations. She crossed the Atlantic Ocean 32 times.

Late in her life, Mamie could still vividly recall President Abraham Lincoln's inauguration. She lived in Illinois then, prior to moving to the Copper Country in 1863. She also recalled the Hancock fire of April 11, 1869, and was living in Lake Linden, Michigan at the time. She stated that she lost her home and possessions in a similar fire there. This was presumably the fire of May 20, 1887, which destroyed 12 city blocks.

Mamie was married to Carl Ferdinand Nelson. She had 16 children, all of whom died relatively young. The 1910 Census indicates that only two of her children were living then. The Nelsons baked pasties in their home at 123 Hancock Street and Carl peddled them locally for many years. He was known throughout the Portage Lake area as "the pasty man" and it was said that his call of "hot pasty" at the train depots was almost as well-known as the conductor's "aboard." Carl died on August 1, 1925, at the age of 88 or 89.

Mamie remained at 123 Hancock Street for many years and became a local celebrity, recounting with consistency the stories of her life, in her advanced age. She was interviewed often and yearned for earlier times. In 1934 she stated, "It's a wicked world. Even the churches have changed. In my day ministers preached on fire and brimstone, and now they even have clubs in their churches. Things aren't what they used to be. When I came to the Copper Country there were Indians (Native Americans) here. Now look at it."

Due to blindness and declining health, Mamie was admitted to the Houghton County Infirmary in October, 1946. She died there on February 25, 1948, shortly after celebrating her 123rd birthday. The medical examiner listed her official cause of death as "old age." News of Mamie's death was reported in papers as far away as New York.

Mamie Nelson was a member of St. Joseph's Church in Hancock. Her funeral service was held at St. Ignatius Church in Houghton, Michigan, and she is buried in Forest Hill Cemetery in nearby Portage Township. Her lifetime was witness to 29 U.S. presidents, the U.S. Civil War, World Wars I and II, and immeasurable social and technological changes.

[Eds. notes: All of the information contained in this chapter appears in official records and published sources. Unfortunately, despite extensive research, few of the details have been substantiated. It is difficult to differentiate fact from fiction in the story of Mamie Nelson's extraordinary life.]

Rex Seeber, Jr.

"Most people call this era the Atomic Age. But I believe there is good reason for calling it the Age of Mathematics and Computation. It is impossible to estimate the ramifications of this development that we are yet to see, not only as scientific computation for engineering and science, but even more as data-processing in all branches of business."[1] Rex Seeber, Jr. wrote those words in 1957. Was he an oracle, a psychic, a seer? No, not in the conventional sense. He was a computing pioneer.

HANCOCK 1863 - 2013

by John S. Haeussler

Robert R. (Rex) Seeber, Jr. was born in Detroit, Michigan, on February 23, 1910. At that time his father, Rex, Sr., was superintendent of the Winona Copper Company. The family resided in Houghton County's Elm River Township. Rex, Sr. was previously an engineer with the Champion Mining Company in Painesdale, Michigan, and the nearby hamlet of Seeberville is named for him.

Rex, Sr.'s employment took him to Dalhousie, New Brunswick, Canada, and later to Chicago, Illinois. Rex, Jr. resided with his mother, Anne (Haddock) Seeber, at 319 Hancock Street. He attended public school in Hancock through 8th grade prior to prepping at Middlesex School in Concord, Massachusetts, from 1924 to 1928. He was admitted to Harvard College, stating on his application that Harvard has "one of the best engineering courses in the country, combined with a desirable element of social, athletic, and literary activity."[2] He received an A.B. in Mathematics from Harvard in 1932.

Seeber immediately found work in the actuarial department of the John Hancock Mutual Life Insurance Company. There he became an expert at using desk calculators and IBM (International Business Machine)

punch-card equipment. In 1942, he became a civilian employee of the U.S. Navy and put his experience to use in Washington, D.C., with the Anti-Submarine Warfare Operations Research Group. He received multiple awards for his contributions to the war effort including the Office of Science Research and Development Certificate of Merit. After learning of the Automatic Sequence Controlled Calculator (ASCC or Harvard Mark I), Seeber requested a transfer to the Harvard Computational Laboratory in Cambridge, Massachusetts, to write programs for the ASCC and to work on the development of a follow-up machine.

IBM funded the construction of the Harvard Mark I and assisted in the engineering effort, yet, to the disappointment of Seeber and others, they received none of the credit when the machine was unveiled in 1944. Upon release from his naval employment, Seeber left the Harvard lab and joined the IBM staff in August, 1945. A member of the Watson Scientific Computing Laboratory at Columbia University, his intention was to build a machine bigger and better than the ASCC. Seeber became the chief architect and co-inventor of IBM's Selective Sequence Electronic Calculator (SSEC). The SSEC was installed on the ground floor of a large Madison Avenue storefront

Seeber became the chief architect and co-inventor of IBM's Selective Sequence Electronic Calculator (SSEC), one of the first computers.

in New York City where it was visible to all passersby on the busy street. It was dedicated to the use of science throughout the world on January 27, 1948, and was operated on a nonprofit basis. It was not operated on Mondays, however. That day was reserved for removing moths from the SSEC's 12,000-plus vacuum tubes. This may be the origin of the computing term "de-bugging!"

One of Seeber's key contributions to the SSEC was to treat instructions as data; thus, its programming could be modified and stored after construction. Stored program ability is the basis for computing; it's a fundamental difference between calculators and computers. Accepting this, it follows that the SSEC was, in fact, one of the first computers.

Among its many applications the SSEC calculated the positions of the moon through 1971, and, although later revised, these calculations formed the groundwork for the course taken by Apollo 11 to reach the moon in July, 1969. It was also utilized by the Los Alamos National Laboratory in early, large-scale applications of Monte Carlo simulation[3]. Seeber was dubbed the "master of the SSEC." He managed the staff, oversaw all programming, and was on site at Madison Avenue to show IBM's prized machine to researchers, dignitaries, and others who dropped by. For a time it was the world's preeminent supercomputer, yet it quickly became obsolete and was dismantled in 1952. The SSEC's legacy includes providing positive publicity for IBM, patent[4] coverage for IBM, and early training for programmers.

While a senior staff member at IBM, Seeber held the title of Associate in Astronomy at Columbia University. He also headed an IBM team of programmers whose many accomplishments include the development of the programming language FORTRAN.

Seeber transferred to IBM's Poughkeepsie, New York, office in 1956, and served as a technical adviser, senior engineer, and computer developer. His area of specialty was associative memory.

Rex Seeber, Jr. married Dorothea Paddock[5] in 1933. They have one daughter, the Reverend Sister Laurian Seeber, who resides in Barre, Vermont. The Seebers divorced in 1952, and Rex, Jr. married Phyllis Lovering in 1955. He retired to La Jolla, California, to escape the winters he had known his entire life. He died in La Jolla on September 9, 1969, and would no doubt be fascinated by today's advances in computing technology that he foresaw over a half century ago.

[1] This quote is from the *Twenty-Fifth Anniversary Report* of the Harvard College Class of 1932. Courtesy of the Harvard University Archives.

[2] This quote is from Seeber's Application for Admission, Harvard College, Harvard Engineering School. Courtesy of the Harvard University Archives.

[3] Monte Carlo methods are statistical simulation techniques used to approximate the probabilities of various outcomes.

[4] Seeber is named on at least 13 U.S. patents and several additional foreign patents.

[5] Dorothea P. Seeber later authored the two-in-one children's book, *A Pup Just for Me / A Boy Just for Me*.

Rex Seeber, Sr.

Estelle Seeber.

Seeber Family
by John S. Haeussler

Rex Seeber, Jr. was not the only member of his immediate or extended Hancock family to achieve notoriety.

Rex Seeber, Sr.
During his employment with the Winona Mining Company, Rex Seeber, Sr. (1879-1957) also served as supervisor of Elm River Township, Michigan. Following his years in the mining industry he headed the Department of Mechanical Engineering at the Michigan College of Mining and Technology (now Michigan Technological University) from 1926 to 1948. He directed the school's Copper Fittings Research Program for many years, resulting in three U.S. and 15 foreign patents, and he advocated for courses and equipment in modern electronic computation. Dr. Seeber led the fundraising efforts for the Memorial Union Building and arranged for funds to buy the first components for an analog computer. Michigan Tech established the Seeber Computational Laboratory in 1958. A cherished faculty member and fundraiser, Dr. Seeber was characterized as brilliant, kind, and straightforward.

Estelle (Hanchette) Seeber
Rex, Sr. married Estelle Hanchette (1887-1958) in 1932. Mrs. Seeber was born in Hancock, where she received her elementary education. She attended Liggett School, Detroit; Vassar College; and, Columbia University, from which she received a B.S. from the Teachers College in 1929. She served nationally and internationally with the Young Women's Christian Association, traveling to France and Belgium for the organization following World War I. Mrs. Seeber was active in multiple civic organizations and was elected president of the Michigan Federation of Women's Clubs on March 19, 1943. Her theme for the 50,000-member organization was "Win the War and Build for Peace." Members were asked to study peace proposals and to prepare for the social and economic conditions that would follow the war's end. In one short period — October 15th through December 31, 1944 — Federation members bought or sold $2,583,670 worth of Treasury bonds toward building a naval air armada. Mrs. Seeber was to oversee the Federation's golden jubilee (50th birthday) celebration in 1945, but the Office of Defense Transportation ordered that there be no conventions. She wrote, "I need not say what a great disappointment it was, but little in comparison to the disappointment of those of us who have been hoping and praying for an early peace." The Seebers resided at 108 Center Street.

Charles Hanchette
Estelle Seeber is the daughter of Charles and Nellie Hanchette. In 1889, Mr. Hanchette organized the Northern Michigan Building and Loan Association, which later became Detroit & Northern Savings, and he served as its first managing officer. A prominent local attorney, Mr. Hanchette was admitted to the bar in 1886, and he served multiple terms as prosecuting attorney in Keweenaw County. In 1889, he partnered with then senator Thomas B. Dunstan to form the law firm of Dunstan & Hanchette. Following Dunstan's death in 1902, Mr. Hanchette partnered with Swaby L. Lawton. The law firm of Hanchette & Lawton represented mining company interests during the Copper Miners' Strike of 1913-1914, including working on behalf of the defendants in the Seeberville murders. The Hanchettes resided at 506 Hancock Street and later at 204 Front Street.

HANCOCK 1863 - 2013

Big Louie Moilanen

by Mary Pekkala

Lauri Moilanen and his wife Anna Kaisa (nee Pyykkönen) left Puolanka, Finland, with their six children and immigrated to the United States around 1890. They first settled in Boston Location, a copper-mining area about five miles north of Hancock. The family later moved to nearby Salo, Michigan, where Lauri had purchased a 40-acre parcel of land from Andrew Johnson, a logging contractor for the Quincy Mining Company. Many landowners in Salo were from the Puolanka area of Finland.

The Moilanen's youngest child, Lauri (Lassi), was born in Aittokylä, Puolanka, Finland, on January 5, 1886, and was four years old when he arrived in America. By the age of nine he was the height of an average man and at age 16 he had reached his maximum height of 8 feet, 3 inches, thus earning him the moniker *Big Louie.*

Louie's notorious height gained him widespread attention. F. M. Sackrider, a Houghton, Michigan businessman and hotel owner, employed him as a special attraction at his hotel. Louie later traveled with the Ringling Brothers Circus, who billed him as the world's tallest man. Tiring of people gawking at him and asking dumb questions, the very shy Louie eventually returned to the farm in Salo to live with his widowed mother.

Louie's unusual height and body shape invited ridicule as well. He had comparatively short legs which caused him to have trouble with balance. As he came to town in his horse-drawn buckboard it was quite a sight. The local boys would stare, follow him along the streets, and wait outside the stores for him.

The Franklin Mine employed Louie on the timber gang, but his height made him awkward at his job. He also tried his hand at bartending, operating a saloon at Tezcuco and Franklin Streets for a brief time. Utilizing his incredible reach, he is said to have served his customers from a seated position at the center of the bar, leaning in either direction to fill his patrons' glasses. But, running a tavern was not a satisfying experience with the constant flow of gawkers. He yearned for the solitude of the Salo farm and returned home once again.

In 1911, Louie was elected justice of the peace for Hancock Township. He served in the position until his death.

Louie suffered from occasional spells which caused erratic behavior and on September 13, 1913, he became seriously ill. He was lodged in the jail because of speculation that he was going insane. Dr. Alfred Labine examined him while in jail and determined that he was suffering from a serious physical illness. He ordered Louie transferred to St. Joseph's Hospital, where he was diagnosed with tubercular meningitis of the brain. On September 16th, while making early morning rounds, a Sister noticed a light on in Louie's room. Checking on her patient, she saw that he was reading the Bible. A short time later she heard a loud noise and found him on the floor unconscious. He died within the hour. An autopsy by Dr. Labine, assisted by Drs. Conrad, Pover, Scallon, Stern, and Turner, confirmed that his death was, in fact, the result of tubercular meningitis.

Big Louie died at the young age of 27. A special casket was ordered from Chicago by the local undertaker, John

Crawford. The manufacturer was so flabbergasted at the size of the casket that he wired the undertaker specifically to verify Louie's measurements. It required eight men to take Louie into the Finnish Evangelical Lutheran Church on Reservation Street where Reverend Matti Pesonen officiated.

The horse-drawn hearse was not large enough to hold Louie's casket, so special transportation was arranged for him on a horse-drawn wagon up the steep road leading to Hancock's Lakeside Cemetery. Sixteen pallbearers carried Louie to a burial plot that a friend had purchased for him.

Louie died with little personal funds to pay his expenses. His sickness took what he had, and the county, along with his friends, paid for his burial.

Even after his death, tales of Big Louie abounded. Rumors persisted that his body had secretly been stolen. Louie's body was exhumed in 1914 by undertaker Crawford and witnessed by authorities who found the giant as he had been buried. Cement was poured over the casket to prevent the theft of his body and to finally lay the rumors and Louie to rest. Now, a century after his death, Big Louie Moilanen is a beloved legend in Hancock and throughout the Copper Country.

Edward Steichen

In the history of American photography a handful of men are considered pioneers. Edward Steichen is at the top of that short list.

HANCOCK 1863 - 2013

by Charles Eshbach

Arriving in Hancock in 1881, Steichen spent the next eight and a half years in this mining boom town on the edge of the frontier. These early years on rutted Quincy Street gave him a sturdy, self-reliant, street-wise independence which was tempered by firm discipline at home. His mother, Marie, was the "guiding and inspiring influence" in Steichen's life. Encouraging and always positive, she "sought to imbue me with her own great strength and fortitude; her deep, warm optimism and human understanding."

This early environment and lifestyle would serve him well in his long career of shaping the art and culture of the 20th century. Among his colleagues and friends were Alfred Stieglitz, Carl Sandburg (his brother-in-law), Henri Matisse, Pablo Picasso, and Auguste Rodin. Steichen was a rebel, independent and self-taught, to those who knew him, but temperamental, ruthless in drive and perfection, and a true humanitarian and visionary to those who worked with him. These attributes helped him become famous on two continents by the age of 25. He went on to make landmark accomplishments, establishing photography as art.

In order to appreciate the influence his years in Hancock had in shaping Steichen, the artist, you need to understand what kind of place Hancock was.

In the 1880s, Hancock was the center of the richest mining region in the world. It was one of several boom towns that had sprung up on the discovery of pure, native copper. At this time, its growth was not keeping up with the thousands of immigrants arriving on ships and trains from the south. As father Jean-Pierre, Marie, and 18-month-old Edward Steichen walked up Tezcuco Street to Quincy Street, they found it a rough and tumble place. Hancock was not a family town. Profane language was common on the street and teenage ruffians bullied naive immigrants while drunken men and bawdy saloon girls spilled out of the growing number of saloons. Nice places to stay were scarce, with several unrelated people often sharing meager housing. The tired Steichens were too weary to consider going any other place and found two cheap rooms to rent. Marie promptly got a job at the general store of Joseph A. Wertin and Sons, and Jean-Pierre went to work in a local mine for $1.70 per day.

Marie was able to keep an eye on young Edward, or leave him with a neighbor, while working at the store. However, with the arrival of a daughter, Lilian, it became more difficult to coordinate childcare with her work schedule. Marie decided to open her own business and have the children with her while she worked. While most Hancock businesses catered to the local miners, few accommodated the women in town. Recognizing this as an opportunity, Marie opened a dress shop.

As Edward grew and entered St. Anne's, a Catholic school just down the street, his father's health failed. Jean-Pierre quit the mine, and Steichen saw his mother

become the main bread-winner. Marie arranged for Jean-Pierre to obtain a clerk position in the Wertin's general store, a much more hospitable environment for his health than the underground copper mines. As Marie's business prospered, the family moved to 321 Quincy Street, over the dress shop.

Marie was stronger than her husband, physically and mentally. She was more aggressive and better at coping with the hardships in the new world. As her dress-making business grew, she saw another venture which would help her growing family. Hancock women were seeing more social and cultural activities with lectures, concerts, and a library. Marie concluded that ladies needed the latest in fashion-able hats. Soon she was busy filling orders, working late into the night.

Jean-Pierre grew stronger after leaving the mine and started a large garden in their backyard. Edward and Lilian soon were de-livering large baskets of produce and flow-ers to customers all over town. Working in the garden with their father produced some of their favorite memories.

When Steichen's 1955 exhibition, "The Family of Man," received such world-wide acclaim, he replied with a story of his childhood in Hancock:

"When work in the copper mines of Han-cock, Michigan, broke my father's health, my mother assumed the responsibilities of bread-winner and opened a millinery shop. In spite of long, tireless hours in her business, she always made time for heart-to-heart conferences with her children. Once, when I was about ten years old, I came home from school, and as I was en-tering the door of her millinery shop, I turned back and shouted into the street, 'You dirty, little kike!' My mother called me over to the counter where she was serving customers and asked me what it was that I had called out. With innocent frankness I repeated the insulting remark. She requested the customers to excuse her, locked the door of the shop, and took me upstairs to our apartment. There, she talked to me quietly and earnestly for a long, long time explaining that all people were alike regardless of race, creed, or color. She talked about the evils of bigotry and intolerance. This was possibly the most important single moment in my growth towards manhood, and it was certainly on that day the seed was sown that, 66 years later, grew into an exhibition called 'The Family of Man.'"

Marie's aim in life was to provide the best for her children, but the Hancock schools - Catholic, Lutheran, and Union - stopped at age 12. This concern led her to consult her priest, Father Edward Jacker, a German immigrant who started St. Anne's Parish. He put her in contact with the Pio Nono College and Catholic Normal School in Milwaukee, Wisconsin. Marie made the hard decision, and one day in 1888, she bade goodbye to her son and put him on the train for Milwaukee. Edward Steichen left his mother's side with a label sewn to his lapel for the priest who would meet him there.

Thus ended Steichen's exposure to Hancock, the rough and rowdy mining town that had molded his independence and free-thinking spirit. Those years prepared him to apply his creative talents on canvas and through the lens. His amazing ability to interpret the American fabric with poignant images, captivating exhibitions in war and peace time, was nurtured in Hancock, giving him the sensitivity which prepared him for his extraordinary career.

His amazing ability to interpret the American fabric with poignant images, captivating exhibitions in war and peace time, was nurtured in Hancock, giving him the sensitivity which prepared him for his extraordinary career.

Marie and Jean-Pierre Steichen; photo by Edward Steichen.

A famous philosopher explains this phenomenon by comparing this immigrant-rich, rapid-growth environment of hard-working people striving for a better life as the same kind of environment and mix of people which fostered the great Renaissance a century before, producing the world's greatest artists, musicians, and world-changers. Steichen, a son of immigrants, is remembered today as a brilliantly original, dramatic, and unforgettable painter, photographer, and communicator who brought mankind into the visual 20th century.

Portrait of My Mother, 1908; photo by Edward Steichen.

Lieutenant Commander Edward Steichen aboard the *U.S.S. Lexington*, 1943.

By the end of its world tour, "The Family of Man" exhibition had been seen, in person, by more than 9,000,000 people.

Edward Steichen with "The Family of Man" exhibit, 1955.

Below is a greatly condensed list of Steichen's career accomplishments:

1879	Born Eduard Jean Steichen on March 27th, in Bivange, Luxembourg
1899	Receives initial recognition as a photographer at Philadelphia, Pennsylvania show
1900	Alfred Stieglitz buys three of Steichen's prints
1900	Travels to Paris, France, to study with Auguste Rodin
1900	Has first showing of 21 prints in London, England
1901	Shows 35 prints in the New School of American Photography exhibition
1901	Is honored as a painter in Paris
1902	Has first one-man show of painting and photographs held at La Maison des Artistes, Paris

Pablo Picasso and Edward Steichen, 1964.

1902	Returns to New York and initiates the first show of art in all media including Rodin's drawings and his photography
1902	Is recognized for his portrait photography, done in his home studio at 291 5th Avenue, Manhattan, New York
1903	Receives "best photo" award in International Exhibition at The Hague, Netherlands
1903	Makes his first color photograph
1904	Makes the image *Pond-Moonlight* at Mamaroneck, New York
1905	Collaborates with Stieglitz to transform his former home studio into the Little Galleries of the Photo-Secession
1906-1917	Introduces America to modern art in numerous multi-media shows

1917	Volunteers and is commissioned first lieutenant in U.S. Army where he develops aerial photographic reconnaissance and earns the Distinguished Service citation from General John J. Pershing
1923	Begins work as chief photographer for *Vogue* and *Vanity Fair*, transforming fashion and advertising photography
1923	Decides to abandon painting as a profession and concentrate solely on photography; burns all of his paintings in his possession
1933	Designs photomurals for the New York State Building at the Chicago World's Fair
1937-1940	Receives the Art Directors Club medal and the silver medal award for his service to advertising
1941-1946	Is invited to establish a unit of photographers to photograph naval aviation; is commissioned lieutenant commander; creates photo exhibition concept "Road to Victory," which gets great reviews; receives honorary M.A. degree from Wesleyan University; supervises U.S. Navy film, *The Fighting Lady*; is named director of U.S. Navy Photographic Institute and is made commander of all Navy combat photography; receives Distinguished Service Medal; organizes exhibition "Power in the Pacific"
1947	Becomes first director of Department of Photography, The Museum of Modern Art, New York
1948	Exhibition "In and Out of Focus" includes photos by 50 photographers in Photo-Secession group
1949	Receives U.S. Camera Achievement Award for the most outstanding contribution to photography by an individual
1949	Develops exhibitions which promote young photographers including Ansel Adams, Edward Weston, Harry Callahan, Eliot Porter, and Dorothea Lange
1949	Creates four major exhibitions
1950	Is asked by the U.S. Navy to oversee Korean War photography
1950	Produces four major exhibits

1951	Creates major exhibition on Korean War and four other shows honoring photographers worldwide
1952	Begins work on signature exhibition, "The Family of Man"
1953	Selects the American section for "The Exhibition of Contemporary Photography: Japan and America," National Museum of Modern Art, Tokyo, Japan
1955	Exhibition "The Family of Man" opens
1955-1962	"The Family of Man" reaps a multitude of awards from photographic and art organizations and is touted as the greatest exhibit ever; travels the world promoting the exhibition and receiving awards; directs the production of several major exhibits every year showcasing young photographers world wide; gives many illustrated lectures and receives dozens of honors and degrees
1961	Honored on his 82nd birthday with the exhibition "Steichen the Photographer" at the Museum of Modern Art
1963	Awarded the Presidential Medal of Freedom by President John F. Kennedy on July 4th
1973	Dies March 25th, at his farm in West Redding, Connecticut
2004	Luxembourg issues Steichen postage stamp on March 16th
2006	A print of 1904's *Pond-Moonlight* sells at auction for $2.9 million, a world record for a photo image; the print is one of three known versions in existence, each hand-made by Steichen by applying layers of light-sensitive gums to the paper to give the impression of color; the other two prints are in museum collections

Lilian Steichen Sandburg

The extraordinary life of Lilian Steichen Sandburg began in Hancock on May 1, 1883. She was born to Jean-Pierre and Marie Kemp Steichen, who emigrated from Luxembourg in 1880. Jean-Pierre worked as a copper miner in a local mine, but when his health deteriorated due to the harsh conditions underground, Marie became the bread-winner. She supported the family with a millinery shop, located below their apartment at 321 Quincy Street. She sold hand-made dresses and hats, having a particular flair for the latter. A testament to her hard work ethic, she often would stay up late into the night preparing items for sale and then do the household chores before opening her shop by 8:00 a.m. Jean-Pierre later found employment again as a clerk in Joseph A. Wertin and Sons' general store on Tezcuco Street.

HANCOCK 1863 - 2013

by Glenn Anderson

Lilian was the Steichen's second child, joining her four-year-old brother, Edward. Lilian and Edward were close while growing up, and she often accompanied him on the streets of Hancock as he sold vegetables grown by their father in a small garden behind their apartment. The Steichen children grew up speaking Luxembourgish at home, but, like many immigrants, they later learned English.

Caught up in the pursuit of the American dream, Marie envisioned great things for her two bright and spirited children. It was clear early on that Edward was a gifted child, and his parents enrolled him at the age of nine in a Catholic school near Milwaukee, Wisconsin. One year later, in 1889, wary of the rough mining town atmosphere which then prevailed in Hancock, and convinced that her son would be a great artist, Marie relocated the family to

be near him in Milwaukee. Marie was quick to open a new millinery shop, and Lilian would receive her education there as well.

Edward Steichen acquired his first camera in 1895, and only one picture turned out from his initial roll of film. It was a photo of his sister Lilian. She was 12 years old, dressed in white, with her long, black hair prominent, seated at a piano with her hands in proper form on the keys. He titled the shot, *My Little Sister*.

Realizing his younger sister's intelligence and spunk, Edward encouraged her to be independent and to find her own destiny in life. Lilian's father, however, urged his daughter to quit high school and work with her mother in the millinery shop. In the end, Lilian listened to her brother's advice and rebelled against her father's wishes.

Lilian and Edward Steichen, 1884.

Edward and Lilian Steichen, 1886.

Lilian Steichen, *My Little Sister*, 1895; photo by Edward Steichen.

Edward and Lilian Steichen, *Self-Portrait with Sister*, 1900; photo by Edward Steichen.

Carl and Lilian Sandburg, 1923; photo by Edward Steichen.

Lilian went off to Chatham, Ontario, Canada, for a year of study she arranged for herself at Ursuline Convent, a Catholic school for girls. In 1900, despite not having graduated from high school, 17-year-old Lilian passed the entrance exams for the University of Illinois. In September, 1901, at a time when very few women attended college, she transferred to the University of Chicago. There she was inducted to Phi Beta Kappa, an academic honors society, and she received a degree in Philosophy, with honors in English and Latin, in 1903.

Around this time the Steichen family moved, with Edward's financial assistance, to a small, four-acre farm near Menomonee Falls, Wisconsin, about 15 miles outside of Milwaukee. At the farm they grew corn and potatoes.

By now Edward Steichen had traveled to New York and Paris, France, and engaged with Alfred Stieglitz on the latter's quarterly journal, *Camera Work*, intended to establish photography as a fine art. Inspired by her brother's success, Lilian began to take her own writing seriously. She often attended concerts and plays in Milwaukee and became interested, along with her mother, in area politics. She volunteered to translate socialist articles and pamphlets from English to German, and German to English, for the Wisconsin Social-Democratic Party. Lilian and Marie were often the only women present at party meetings.

Beginning in September, 1904, Lilian taught for two years in Valley City, North Dakota. She then went to Princeton, Illinois, to teach high school literature and expression. On December 29, 1907, Carl Sandburg went to Milwaukee to begin work as an organizer for the Wisconsin Social-Democratic Party, just as Lilian was ending her Christmas visit to her parents'

farm that same day. En route back to Princeton, she stopped at party headquarters to see friends and, by chance, met the new party organizer.

After they talked for a while, Lilian gave Carl her address in Princeton, and he promised to send her some of his writing. On June 12, 1908, following a six-month, whirlwind courtship by letters, they were married in Milwaukee. Carl was 30; Lilian was 25. They were together only twice during their courtship, so it was through the written word that they became intimately acquainted.

During their courtship, Carl began to call his future wife *Paula*, derived from *Paus'l*, an affectionate nickname for girls in Luxembourg that was used by her family. Lilian's birth certificate reads *Mary A.* She was baptized *Anna Marie Elizabeth*[1] by Father Edward Jacker at Hancock's St. Anne's Church on May 5, 1883. Her mother called her *Lily*, likely short for *Elizabeth*. When she went to school, Lily elected to use the name *Lilian*. In one of Carl's love poems to Lilian, he aptly called her a woman of a million names.

After the wedding, Carl worked on Eugene Deb's campaign for president. He desired to be a writer, but became discouraged. While he was traveling for Deb's campaign, Lilian wrote to him, "The poems are great, Carl. It would be all wrong to give them up. We must give the Poet every chance! If we can only assure ourselves leisure for this— you will arrive."

In addition to encouragement, Lilian supplied inspiration. Carl wrote in one of his early letters to her, "I would rather be a poem like you than write poems. I would rather embody the big things as you do than carve or paint or write them. You inspire art—and that's living!"

Carl wrote in one of his early letters to her, "I would rather be a poem like you than write poems."

Following Deb's failed bid for the presidency, Carl wrote for several Milwaukee-area newspapers. When socialists took office in 1910, Carl became secretary to Milwaukee Mayor Emil Seidel. During this period he decided to focus on his own writing. With Lilian's continued support, they formed a lifelong creative union.

Although they originally planned to co-author a book, the Sandburgs agreed that Carl would have a career as a writer and that Lilian would help create an environment to make that possible. While assuming different roles, they would remain equals. Lilian focused on maintaining their home and tending to their animals, primarily chickens at this time. Carl was given ample opportunity to cultivate his talent and he flourished.

Carl's career is highlighted by three Pulitzer Prizes: two in poetry for *The Complete Poems of Carl Sandburg* and *Cornhuskers*; and, one in biography for *Abraham Lincoln: The War Years*. Lilian often reviewed his manuscripts and made editorial suggestions. Carl referred to her as a literary stylist and pundit.

The Sandburgs lived in Michigan and Illinois before purchasing Connemara Farm, a 246-acre rural estate in Flat Rock, North Carolina, in 1945. Lilian utilized the space to raise champion dairy goats.

The Sandburgs had three daughters: Margaret, Janet, and Helga. Carl died in 1967, at the age of 89, and Lilian died on February 18, 1977, at the age of 93.

Following Carl's death, Lilian transferred Connemara Farm to the U.S. government. It is maintained by the National Park Service as a National Historic Site, and the goats have been designated an historic herd.

Carl Sandburg spent his life championing social justice and the American people through his writing and singing. Anna Marie Elizabeth Lilian Paula Steichen Sandburg was there throughout it all. She was his booster, confidante, lover, partner, and muse — leading an exciting life in politics, society, and the literary world that began on the village streets of Hancock.

[1] Lilian's baptismal record reads *Anna Maria Elizabet Steichen* and lists her parents as *Joannes* and *Maria*. Jacker hailed from southern Germany, Jean-Pierre was of French heritage, and Marie was of Teutonic descent. They all spoke German, but it's difficult to definitively discern their English intent. Making an educated guess, *Anna* corresponds to the *A.* on Lilian's birth certificate; *Maria* is correctly *Marie*, for her mother; and *Elizabet* is *Elizabeth* or *Elisabeth* – the name of Jean-Pierre's sister, mother, and grandmother.

HANCOCK 1863 - 2013

Maude Sincock Roberts

by Charles Eshbach

"I am saved but I have lost everything. I must however be thankful for my life. I have not a penny and no clothes. I was thrown on board a little boat in my night dress and boots. I had no stockings on. We were in this little boat in the middle of the ocean for six hours, and I was nearly frozen when we were picked up. I shall be a pretty sight when we land." This is the opening statement of the letter Maude Sincock wrote to her mother from the rescue ship *Carpathia*, after surviving the wreck of the steamship *Titanic* on its maiden voyage from England to New York.

Maude was on her way to Hancock with her mother's relatives, Mrs. Agnes Davies and her sons John Davies (then eight years old) and Joseph (Joe) Nicholls (19 years old), who were headed for Mohawk, Michigan. They had been booked on another ship, but due to a coal miners' strike, that ship transferred their coal and passengers to the *Titanic*. Maude's father and older sister had previously immigrated to Hancock. Maude left her mother and seven siblings in Halsetown, St. Ives, Cornwall, England, and traveled to Southampton to board the *Titanic*. She boarded at noon and was very excited to be sharing a cabin in second class with Alice Phillips. As the *Titanic* pulled away, lunch was served. "It was such a lovely day and I found the other passengers very friendly," Maude remembered. "The next days were wonderful, as the weather was excellent and the ship was beautiful."

On the night of April 14, 1912, just three days before Maude's 21st birthday, the *Titanic* struck an iceberg. Maude recalled, "I was in bed when we hit. It did not sound too bad, but soon a steward came along banging on every door calling, 'Everyone on deck with lifebelts.' I got up quickly and put a raincoat over my nightgown." As she stepped out into the hallway, people were

asking the steward if the ship was going to sink. He said that it was only a precaution. "I went to the elevator but the lift boy was gone. I then climbed six decks up to the lifeboat deck. The deck was crowded with people pushing and shoving trying to find friends. I stayed put on the rail and watched the lifeboats being filled."

Maude waited her turn and was helped into the boat marked 'number 11.' The boat was filled with 25 people and lowered over the side into the ocean. "As I looked back on deck, I saw the firemen coming up in their dirty work clothes, which meant it was really bad. The ocean was calm. The air was cold. A sailor told me, 'She's going fast.' Looking back I could see the lights disappearing as the bow sank down, water pouring into the open portholes." Maude also described how the flares overhead lit the scene in red light as they rowed away from the stricken vessel.

"As the ship sank and broke apart I could hear screams from the men on board and then the loud explosions as the boilers blew." Later, Maude wrote her mother, "Mrs. Davies and her son John Morgan are saved, but we have seen nothing of Joe. We think he was drowned." Joe's floating body was recovered later with Maude's wristwatch in his overcoat pocket. He must have returned to the cabin and picked up the ladies' loose jewelry.

After six hours of paddling around among the icebergs the rescue ship *Carpathia* was seen approaching. Maude remembered it took a long time for each person to be hoisted up the side of the ship from the lifeboats. On deck the people of the *Carpathia* were very nice, getting the survivors warm, dry clothes and food. Maude wrote, "I don't know what I shall do when I get to New York? I am frightened to death nearly, and I am afraid I shall catch my

> "As the ship sank and broke apart I could hear screams from the men on board and then the loud explosions as the boilers blew."

death of cold by the time I get to Hancock. I will write again as soon as possible to tell you more news. I do not know where they will put us when we get to New York."

On arrival in New York, Maude, Mrs. Davies, and her son John were instructed to wait until the White Star Line gave them money to reach their destinations. They stayed with a host family that was very nice and quick to help them. Several days later, Maude arrived in Hancock after a long train ride and was very happy to see her father and sister.

Maude soon was asked to appear at the Orpheum Theatre in Hancock to tell the story of her rescue. Later she traveled to theatres in Marquette and Ishpeming, Michigan, sharing her story.

Maude married Arling Roberts on April 2, 1918. Arling was a dock worker in Ripley, Michigan. Maude worked at Michigan Bell as a telephone operator. They had three children, Virginia (Piiponen), June (Talbot), and Francis. Maude was active in the First Methodist Church of Hancock and a longtime member of the Women's Society of Christian Service. She was also active in the women's auxiliary of the Veterans of Foreign Wars.

Maude Sincock Roberts, *Titanic* survivor, spent her later years in senior housing in Hancock. She died on May 21, 1984. Her favorite pastimes were visiting family and baking pasties and saffron buns.

HANCOCK 1863 - 2013

A. J. Scott

by John S. Haeussler

Characterized as clear-sighted, energetic, and keenly alive to the questions of his day, A. J. Scott left an indelible mark on Hancock. His name survives today on the Scott Building and Scott Street, but he was involved in much more.

Archibald J. Scott was born on January 24, 1848, near London, Ontario, Canada. His parents died while he was an infant, and he was raised by an uncle, Donald D. Scott. A railroad contractor, Donald's work took him to New York, Vermont, and Ohio, with young Archie in tow. They settled in Watertown, Wisconsin, in 1855, and A. J. Scott attended public school there.

Several published sources state that Scott enlisted in 1863, at age 15, in the 52nd Wisconsin Volunteer Infantry, and that he served as an orderly under his uncle, Donald, participating in U.S. Civil War campaigns throughout the south that culminated in Major General William Tecumseh Sherman's March to the Sea. He then re-enlisted in 1865 and went west, guarding those employed in the construction of the Union Pacific Railroad. Accounts of Scott's involvement from 1863 forward are likely accurate, although the specifics of his enlistment differ from above. Donald D. Scott was a captain, major, and eventually lieutenant colonel in the 17th Wisconsin Volunteer Infantry, which was part of the first brigade to enter Vicksburg, Mississippi, upon the fall of that city on July 4, 1863. Lt. Col. Scott and the 17th Regiment were also with Maj. Gen. Sherman when the Georgia cities of Atlanta and Savannah were captured in late 1864. A. J. does not appear on the roster of the 17th Regiment, but it's plausible, especially given that they represented each other's only immediate family, that he traveled with the unit in 1863 and 1864 as a non-enlisted orderly of Donald's. Official records indicate that A. J. Scott

enlisted with the 52nd Regiment on April 10, 1865, and served as a guard to Union Pacific Railroad workmen in St. Louis and Holden, Missouri, prior to mustering out in Leavenworth, Kansas, on July 28, 1865.

Scott moved to Houghton County, Michigan, in 1866, gaining employment in a saw mill. He established residence in Hancock in 1867 and clerked for druggist Manus J. McGurrin. He worked there until the store was destroyed in the great fire of April 11, 1869. Shortly thereafter, Scott opened a small drugstore of his own. The initial location of Scott's business is believed to be at the corner of Hancock and Tezcuco Streets. The store grew substantially and, at 210 Quincy Street, became one of the best-stocked in the Upper Peninsula.

In 1870, Scott partnered with Alex Hamilton to produce Hancock's first newspaper, *The Hancock Times*. The initial November 12, 1870 issue announced that it was to be "published semi-occasionally, by Hamilton, Scott & Co." An ad for Edward Ryan's dry goods appeared in the first issue. Marriages were announced under the banner, "Slaughter of Innocents." The paper was described as plucky and spicy. Its short run ended on February 17, 1872, with a "Personal Tale of Blasted Hopes."

Around this same time, Scott worked with Christian Broemer to form Hancock's first fire department. He remained active with the department for many years and helped organize the Upper Peninsula Firemen's Association, for which he served as president.

Scott was named supervisor of Hancock Township in 1879, a position he held through 1903. This granted him a seat on the Board of Supervisors of Houghton County, where he was often the lone

Democrat. He was also the village assessor and village treasurer in the late 1870s and/or early 1880s. A. J. Scott next served Hancock as supervisor of the water works. He oversaw installation of the first pumping station in 1890, and a new and larger pump in 1902.

Scott was elected village president in 1897. The following year he was prominently mentioned as a candidate for the Democratic nomination for state representative. He was also reported to have left the party due to a disagreement over the best monetary system. Scott favored the single gold standard at the time, while others preferred the double standard, under which both gold and silver were legal tender. In the October 12, 1898, edition of *The Milwaukee Journal*, Scott affirmed that he was still a Democrat. He stated, "I will not desert my party, but stay with it and assist in bringing it over to my way of thinking." Scott did not run for the state legislature that year, but he did in 1900, losing to George W. Rulison by a nearly three-to-one margin. This was a fairly typical spread for the area in favor of Republican candidates at the time.

For six years, Scott faced little or no opposition for the position of village president.

The Scott Building
by Susan Burack and John S. Haeussler

The Scott Hotel opened for business in August, 1906. One of the finest hotels in the Upper Peninsula, the five-story landmark was a project that almost didn't happen.

In 1905, the residents of Hancock desired a hotel of which the community would be proud and "a piece of land to be used as a public amusement place." Houghton, Michigan businessman F. M. Sackrider proposed to accommodate both wishes by selling Hancock's Driving Park to the city and building a first-class hotel at the corner of Quincy and Reservation Streets. This was a highly visible and viable location, being adjacent to the popular Kerredge Theatre, which opened in 1902.

Former mayor A. J. Scott had previously managed the Driving Park, a sizeable property at the west end of Ingot Street which hosted horse races and other events, and he was a strong proponent of Sackrider's proposal.

A special election was held on July 10, 1905, and Hancock residents overwhelmingly approved a plan in which the city would purchase the Driving Park for $18,000 and Sackrider would erect a hotel for not less than $50,000. But, within a matter of days it appeared that Sackrider was having cold feet. By the end of the month, when the city refused to purchase the Driving Park until the construction of the hotel was completed, the deal was off.

Little news was reported on the project for over a month, until Scott announced in September that he had purchased the Driving Park from Sackrider and was prepared to work with the city on the same terms. City officials looked favorably upon Scott's offer. The Driving Park was purchased and construction of the hotel was immediately commenced. It was completed the following year and was a fine credit to both Scott and the city.

The building remained a hotel until the 1970s, when it was occupied by a hardware store. As time passed the upper floors filled with debris and pigeons. The building was in danger of being structurally compromised and there was concern that this historically significant anchor of downtown would become a parking lot.

Local developer Mike Lahti purchased the Scott Building, as it is now known, in 2005. Partnering with the city and utilizing grants and loans from the Michigan State Housing Development Authority, in addition to private funds, Lahti oversaw a $4-$5 million renovation of the building. It reopened in 2007, with 28 one- and two-bedroom apartments on the upper four floors and retail space for three businesses on the lower level.

The renovation preserved the original woodwork and many architectural features including the grand stairway. An elevator, sprinkler system, common areas, laundry rooms, fire alarms, and smoke detectors brought the building to code. Interior rooms, looking onto an airshaft, became storage spaces.

Residents, aged 55 years and older, enjoy a location central to downtown. Several of the spacious apartments are handicapped-accessible. The units include new kitchens with refrigerators, stoves, garbage disposals, and dishwashers. Heat, water, trash, and plowed parking are included in the income-based rent.

Now in its second century, the Scott Building remains a downtown anchor and is again viewed by the community with pride.

HORSE RACES
AT
HANCOCK
DRIVING
PARK
JULY 4-5, 1901.

Program of Races:

JULY 4.	JULY 5.
1:00 minute class. $100	2:50 minute class $150
2:25 " " 200	2:30 minute class 180
2:40 " " 150	Free for all 225

Money divided 50, 25, 15, and 10 per cent. of purse. Entrance fee five per cent. in all races, and five per cent. additional from winners.

Races to begin at 2 p. m. sharp each day.

Entrance, 5 per cent. in all races, and 5 per cent. additional from winners.

The Club reserves the right to declare all races off on account of bad weather or track, or other unavoidable cause, in which case the entrance paid will be refunded. Also reserves the right to change the order of the programme.

American Association Rules to govern all harness races, with exceptions as herein contained.

We reserve the right of substituting three races, if thought best by the Association.

Horses may be named in two or more classes, but will not be held for more than one entrance unless one or more days intervene between races.

GOOD MUSIC FURNISHED

A. J. Scott sold the Driving Park to the city and erected the Scott Hotel.

A. J. Scott left an indelible mark on Hancock.

This changed in 1903, when Henry L. Baer, the nephew of previous village president Jacob Baer, mounted a stern challenge. Henry L. Baer was responsible for collecting the petition signatures requesting the village council to take the necessary steps to become a city. Scott was hesitant to run for a seventh one-year term as village president, but he also favored the city proposition and decided to run for re-election and to participate in establishing Hancock as a city. Baer was favored in a pre-election caucus, but on March 9th, Scott retained his position by a count of 596 to 438. The citizens were also overwhelmingly in favor of cityhood, the vote being 757 to 150. The election was followed by a night of revelry, with Scott being carried down Quincy Street on the shoulders of his supporters. During the bedlam a false fire alarm was received from the box at Quincy and Tezcuco Streets, and with the noise of the celebration drowning the sound of the fire bell, the Scott throng was nearly run over by the horse team pulling the hose cart. Three men were struck by the horses, and one was rendered unconscious.

Hancock's declaration of incorporation was received and filed by Secretary of State Fred S. Warner on March 16th, making Hancock the first city in the Copper Country. Many expected another leadership battle between Scott and Baer, but Baer declared that the result was decided in the village elections and that he would not seek the mayorship. On April 6, 1903, Scott was elected the first mayor of Hancock.

The following year witnessed Hancock's first partisan election, and the first in several years without A. J. Scott on the ballot. On March 11, 1904, he told *The Daily Mining Gazette*, "I believe that I have had conferred on me all the politi-

cal honors I am entitled to." With Scott stepping aside, Republican Thomas Coughlin defeated Citizens' candidate John Funkey. Scott's retirement from politics was short-lived, however.

In 1905, Scott challenged Coughlin for the Republican Party nomination as mayor. Coughlin easily won the nomination and, having also been endorsed by the Citizens' Party, he retained his position.

Scott again ran for the Republican nomination in 1906. Construction of the Scott Hotel was ongoing at the time. In reporting on his candidacy, *The Daily Mining Gazette* called Scott "a splendid chief executive" based on his past performance. Scott was unopposed on the Republican ticket and on April 3, 1906, he was elected mayor over Citizens' candidate John F. Ryan. Scott was elected to two additional terms, serving as mayor of Hancock from 1906 through 1909.

There was some thought that Scott would continue leading Hancock beyond 1909, but that didn't happen. He told *The Daily Mining Gazette* in late March of that year, "No, I am not going to be a candidate for mayor. The party will be able to decide on some good man for the place. I have had the position long enough." The good man who succeeded Scott was W. Frank James.

Scott was involved with several financial organizations in the early 20th century. He was vice president of the First National Bank of Hancock for many years, and he served as a director of the Hancock Loan, Mortgage, and Insurance Company and the Superior Trust Company, which consolidated with the Superior National Bank of Hancock in 1941. He also was president of Hancock's Park Brewing Company. Known for constructing around 20 houses in Hancock, Scott's grandest structure was

Hancock First National Base Ball Club, circa 1870. **Back row**: John Bittenbender, Albert A. Brockway, William Harry, and Joseph Johnson. **Front row**: James Walls Trembath, Archibald J. Scott, Thomas D. Meads, John T. V. Trembath, and Otto Charles Kunath.

the Scott Hotel, which opened in 1906 as a monument to Hancock's size and importance.

On June 12, 1880, Scott married Sally Clause, of Philadelphia, Pennsylvania. Mrs. Scott was the niece of Hancock's Roland H. Brelsford, an officer of the Mineral Range Railroad Company, county clerk, and village treasurer. The wedding was presided over by Edmund R. Stiles in Hancock. The Scotts had

five children: Archie, Walter, Florence (Flossie), Lillian, and Jean. The two boys died in infancy. Having originally resided on site at the drugstore, the Scotts later moved to 209 Hancock Street.

Archibald J. Scott died of a stroke on March 8, 1915, in Milwaukee, Wisconsin. He is buried in Hancock's Lakeside Cemetery. His legacy as a Hancock business and civic leader continues to this day.

Hancock following April 11, 1869, fire

Kerredge Theatre fire, 1959.

The Hancock Volunteer Fire Department
by Mark Dennis

In 1864, Hancock's first "bucket brigade" fire company was formed with Edward Guck as its chief. This group of men met regularly in one of the local taverns. They had no fire hall to call their own, and they lacked an adequate water supply and the hoses and other equipment necessary, including buckets, to properly respond in the event of a fire.

On April 11, 1869, a major fire burned the eastern three quarters of Hancock. This fire highlighted the need for a more dedicated and organized fire department, so by 1872, A. J. Scott had formed a group of about fifty men to fight fires in the town. They held regular meetings in Germania Hall, later called Lincoln Hall, which was destroyed in a spectacular fire on December 4, 1966. Christian Broemer was one of the group's organizers and he served for many years as its chief. In 1882, the village council disbanded this unit and organized a new, more efficient company of up to 20 men, led by Chief A. J. Scott. This group formed what is now the Hancock Volunteer Fire Department.

The first fire apparatus, a "hand pump" fire wagon, was purchased in 1871. A two-horse team was needed to haul the wagon. The city didn't own any teams, so when the bell rang in the fire tower, the first privately owned team of horses to arrive got the job and was paid $10 per call. Competition became so fierce among team owners that the city soon reduced the rate to $5 per call.

In 1873, a two-cylinder steam fire engine made by Colis Brothers was purchased. About 2,500 feet of hose was also purchased at that time. In 1875, a new, sturdy, wooden-frame, two-story fire hall with a bell tower was constructed at the intersection of Quincy and Reservation Streets. A new water supply was also provided utilizing water from Portage Lake, cisterns on the hillside and on corners of the main street, and two water systems, one of which was dedicated to fire protection.

In 1898, the city bought a parcel of property located at 399 Quincy Street from the Quincy Mining Company and built a new city hall, police department, and fire department. Two teams of horses were also purchased for the fire department. An alarm system was installed throughout the city with numbered alarm boxes placed at various street corners to aid in the location of fires. Many citizens knew the block numbers and would rush to the scene following a siren to view the action.

Horse teams and fire wagons were eventually eliminated when more modern fire trucks were purchased, one of the first being a 1933 Studebaker. The department has had a number of trucks over the years, with the current group being two pumper engines and an aerial ladder/platform. A new, modern, brick fire hall was dedicated on December 19, 1997, at 900 Ethel Avenue, complete with a large parking lot, four truck bays, a storage room with a breathing air compressor system, a large meeting room, a mechanical room, men's and women's locker and shower rooms, a kitchen area, and a sauna. This facility is in use today.

The Hancock Volunteer Fire Department is trained in ice rescues and it responds to many other types of emergencies throughout the area as well. As part of the Copper Country Firefighters Association Mutual Aid Agreement, a close relationship has been established with many other local fire departments in order to coordinate collective equipment and manpower dispatch to emergencies throughout the area. The current roster has 22 firefighters, all volunteers.

Edmund R. Stiles Grand Army of the Republic Post No. 174

by Philip N. Parks and Roland Burgan

When the U.S. Civil War ended in 1865, soldiers and sailors returned to their homes, many wishing to forget their terrible experiences of war. Some discarded their uniforms and weapons and attempted to put their military time behind them as they returned to a familiar way of life. However, after a few years the Soldiers and Sailors Association of the Upper Peninsula of Michigan was organized. Veterans from Baraga, Houghton, Keweenaw, Marquette, and Ontonagon counties met on September 23, 1879, and formed the nucleus of the new organization. The first officers included Edmund R. Stiles as chaplain.

The Soldiers and Sailors Association held four annual meetings in July in various Copper Country communities: 1880 in Calumet, 1881 in Hancock, 1882 in Lake Linden, and 1883 in Houghton. The group was rather loosely organized and a division arose around sentiment that membership should be restricted to only those who saw active service during the war years.

In August, 1883, local Civil War veterans gathered to organize a Grand Army of the Republic (GAR) post in Hancock. The GAR was a fraternal organization benefitting surviving Union Civil War veterans and honoring those lost in battle. It was founded nationally in Decatur, Illinois, in April, 1866, by Benjamin Franklin Stephenson. Membership peaked at just fewer than 500,000 in 1890.

The new GAR post in Hancock was chartered as Superior Post No. 174 with at least 15 members. Initial officers included Commander James Ross and Adjutant A. J. Scott. Shortly after forming, the post was renamed the Edmund R. Stiles Post No. 174, to honor a fallen comrade.

Edmund Root Stiles was born in Clarksfield, Ohio, on July 12, 1834. He came to Hancock in 1877 to pastor the First Congregational Church, located at the southwest corner of Hancock and Tezcuco Streets. A member of the 7th Ohio Volunteer Infantry, Stiles was captured on August 16, 1861, at the Battle of Cross Lanes in Nicholas County, Virginia (now West Virginia). He was held for nine months at prisons in Richmond, Virginia; New Orleans, Louisiana; and, Salisbury, North Carolina, prior to being exchanged. Edmund R. Stiles died in Hancock on January 13, 1881, as a result of wounds received during the war.

Although some veterans in the Copper County never became affiliated with it, membership in the Edmund R. Stiles Post reached a high of 93. The post closed in 1937 when its last member, Frank Richards of Ripley, Michigan, died.

The GAR was dissolved nationally following the death of its last member, Albert Woolson, in Duluth, Minnesota, in 1956.

Edward Ryan

It's a long, long way from Tipperary to Hancock, and one finds a far different world at the western end of Lake Superior than one does in south central Ireland. For one man, who made that journey as a child, it ultimately involved business success and recognition as a leader, first among his fellow Irish Catholic immigrants in their new home, but later, respect and recognition by the larger community as well. While far from typical of the lives of Irish immigrants to either the United States or Michigan's Copper Country in the middle of the 19th century, Edward Ryan's life is an example of the promise America held for some and the possibilities that existed for a few to succeed beyond their wildest dreams or hopes. When he died in December of 1900, both the Houghton and Calumet newspapers referred to him as the "Merchant Prince of the Copper Country." The evening paper reported his death and followed with stories of his remarkable career, services to the community, and funeral. He was a man of many accomplishments and successes with significant impacts.

HANCOCK 1863 - 2013

by William H. Mulligan, Jr.

Note: This is an abbreviated version of Dr. Mulligan's, 'The Merchant Prince of the Copper Country: one immigrant's American success story' published in the *Tipperary Historical Journal 2004*. It is reprinted here with permission of the author.

Edward Ryan was born in County Tipperary, Ireland, on April 22, 1840, the son of John and Margaret Cuddihy Ryan. In 1844, the Ryans emigrated from Ireland to Wiota, Lafayette County, in the lead-mining district of southwestern Wisconsin. The Ryans, thus, were not part of the massive migration triggered by Ireland's Great Famine. Instead, they came during the last years of the less frenzied and more structured earlier emigration. Families such as the Ryans emigrated as units with sufficient resources to move away from the east coast cities already associated with immigrant slums and ghettos.

In 1854, Edward Ryan moved to Houghton to live with his brother, John C., who apparently had already relocated there. John C. and another brother, William, worked in the copper mines and soon became well known in the region as mine captains and later mine superintendents - men with prestigious, responsible positions in the mining community. One of John C.'s sons, William, served as sheriff of Houghton County in the 1880s and another, John D., ultimately became head of both the Anaconda Copper Mining and Montana Power companies and was one of the wealthiest, most powerful men in America in the early decades of the twentieth century.

Surprisingly, considering his family background, Edward Ryan initially did not work underground in the copper mines. After different kinds of employment and with very little formal education, in 1857, he took a job with Ransom Shelden, one of the most successful pioneer

businessmen of the Copper Country. At first, young Ryan led a team of horses hauling new merchandise up the hill from the dock on Portage Lake to Shelden's store. Later, he made deliveries, traveling about the area in a horse-drawn cart to the many small mining camps and locations around Houghton, before finally becoming a clerk in Shelden's general store. By all accounts he was a personable, well-liked young man. These qualities sped his advancement to the position of clerk. His relationship with Shelden was a critical and recurring factor in his early successes.

In 1862, Edward Ryan, then a 22-year-old store clerk, an immigrant with a very limited education, and an Irish Catholic Democrat, ran for sheriff in what had been a heavily Republican area previously. While issues of the local newspapers from the time of the campaign no longer survive, the editor's reaction to Ryan's initial days in office suggest that he did not garner much, if any, support from that quarter. Instead, opposition most likely focused on his ethnic and religious loyalties, which had already become irretrievably intertwined in the United States. In a series of articles, J. R. Devereuax, editor and publisher of *The Portage Lake Mining Gazette*, made it clear he was not happy with Ryan's victory, or with the prospect of an Irish Catholic sheriff in Houghton County. In the January 17, 1863, edition he wrote:

"Sheriff Ryan, we are happy to say, has thus far disappointed the many predictions we have heard made that when he came into office, the Irish would be allowed to do as they pleased — rule the town perhaps — but the prophets have all proved false for the Sheriff and all his prominent friends are laboring hard and earnestly to make their countrymen keep the peace — and they have done well, considering

the provocation they have had to act otherwise."

In 1864, instead of seeking re-election, Ryan opened his own general merchandise store in Hancock with $2000. For a time, his brother William, who provided additional capital, was a partner. Ransom Shelden also financially backed his former clerk.

Significantly, Ryan opened his store in Hancock, not in Houghton, where he would have been in direct competition with Shelden. After a short time, Ryan bought out his brother's share and William returned to mining as an agent, his career eventually taking him far from the Copper Country.

Due to the rapid growth of the Quincy Mining Company, by the early 1860s, Hancock had a large and rapidly growing Irish population. Hancock was a community in which ethnicity was important — Ryan's business rivals were native-born, German, English, and later 'Austrian' [1] merchants. Interestingly, each store had clerks from a variety of ethnic groups judging from the manuscript population schedules.

Houghton and Calumet newspapers referred to him as the "Merchant Prince of the Copper Country."

The 1865 discovery of the Calumet conglomerate lode resulted in the development of extensive mines and the growth of a sizeable population there. Taking advantage of a new opportunity, three years later, Ryan opened a second general merchandise store in Red Jacket Village. As in Hancock, a member of each of Calumet's major ethnic groups operated a general store. Ryan's was one of the largest, if not the largest.

Ryan's business career was not without serious reverses and challenges. In 1869, a devastating fire destroyed his Hancock store. Within days he was back in business in St. Patrick's Hall, the building erected by the benevolent society formed by Hancock's Irish community in 1860. Ryan quickly rebuilt his store on Quincy, the village's main business street. In 1870, another fire leveled his Calumet store. It, too, was quickly rebuilt. Despite these setbacks, he was already one of the wealthiest men in Hancock. He and his wife had a servant (Irish-born), and one account refers to him as the "leading merchant" in the copper regions with an inventory averaging $120,000. His travels, whether on business or pleasure, were regularly noted in the papers. His children attended Catholic boarding schools after elementary school in Hancock. His daughters were educated at convent schools in St. Louis, Missouri, and South Bend, Indiana. His sons attended the University of Notre Dame.

With the success of his general stores, Ryan sought investments in other ventures. In 1865, when his mentor Ransom Shelden organized the First National Bank of Houghton, he named Ryan a director. In 1880, Ryan organized the Lake Superior Native Copper Works, which smelted copper and rolled sheet copper. Also in 1880, he created the Hancock Copper Mining Company, arranging for eastern capital to

help underwrite the venture, and operated the mine with his brother, John C., as mine superintendent, until 1885.

In 1886, Edward Ryan founded the First National Bank of Calumet and served as its president until his death. He remained a director of the First National Bank of Houghton and was a shareholder, from its beginning, in the Superior Savings Bank, later the Superior National Bank and Trust Company. He co-founded and served as vice president of the Peninsular Electric Light & Power Company.

In 1883, Ryan, Capt. Nathan Moore, and others, including John C., conducted explorations on the Gogebic Iron Range and operated several successful iron mines there. They were among the pioneers in operating iron mines in that part of Michigan. A significant number of Irish miners from the Copper Country went to the Gogebic Range and worked in Ryan's mines. At the time of his death, Ryan had a substantial number of shares in the Quincy Mining Company, known as "Old Reliable" for the regularity of its dividend payments. Over the course of his business career, Ryan had diversified his economic interests while also helping develop the Copper Country economy.

Ryan did not devote all of his energy to his multiple business ventures. He served on the Houghton County Board of Supervisors from Hancock Township for nine years, most of them as chairman, and he served nine consecutive years as Hancock village president, after a briefer term in the same office.[2] Beginning in 1871, he was a member of the Hancock school board and remained prominent in Hancock community school affairs for 28 years. A public elementary school built in Hancock in 1897 bears his name.[3] He was a member and leader, by 1863, of the St. Patrick's

Edward Ryan store.

Hancock Copper Mining Company.

Benevolent Society, and later of the Ancient Order of Hibernians, when the Hancock Division was organized in 1881.

Ryan was a devout and active Catholic, first in Hancock's St. Anne's Parish. Later, it was renamed and rededicated as St. Patrick's, after the German and French-Canadian parishioners established their own parish. He and his wife were known as generous financial supporters of the Catholic Church, community charities, and needy Irish families. The Bishop traveled nearly one hundred miles in December to preside at Ryan's funeral mass. His eldest daughter, Margaret, became a nun in the Sisters of St. Joseph of Carondelet, which staffed the parish schools in Hancock as well as the hospital.

After he was sheriff, Ryan never sought elected office outside the village of Hancock, but he remained active in Democratic Party politics. His influence in the party extended well beyond the Copper Country. He developed a reputation as a forceful and effective stump speaker for Democratic candidates, frequently debating with Jay Hubbell, a Republican who was elected to Congress from the Upper Peninsula. In 1876, Ryan was elected as a delegate to the Democratic National Convention and served as a delegate again in 1892.

In 1865, he married Alice Cuddihy of Houghton. They resided at 221 Hancock Street. Edward and Alice had ten children, nine of whom survived him. Margaret and Alice died within months of one another in 1896. Ryan's own health began to decline shortly thereafter.

Edward Ryan died in Hancock early in the morning on December 14, 1900, at the age of 60, of acute gastritis. He had been in poor health for several years, cutting back on first his public, and then his business, activities. As he was withdrawing from public life, the local papers featured articles extolling his multifaceted community service over many years. He was widely respected, not only for his economic success, but for his community service and his (and his wife's) generosity to their church, the local Irish, and to the people of Hancock and Calumet. The personable, likeable young man who had worked in Shelden's store when the Copper Country was young did not change much, apparently, as he accumulated wealth and honors over the years. For many, Edward Ryan represented the dream the Irish community shared and which he, if not they, had fully achieved.

[1] 'Austrians' were generally Slovenes or others from the Austro-Hungarian Empire confusingly lumped together.

[2] This is the second longest consecutive run as village president or city mayor in Hancock history, trailing only Norman D. Starrett (1925-1936).

[3] This property is now known as the Ryan Center.

HANCOCK 1863 - 2013

Jacob Gartner

by David Mac Frimodig

Note: This article was originally published in *Keweenaw
Character: The Foundation of
Michigan's Copper Country*
under the heading 'A Ped-
dler's Legacy' in 1990. It has
been updated and is reprinted
here with permission of the
Frimodig family and the publisher, the Houghton County
Historical Society.

Walking to work has become some-what of a bragging event in today's physical fitness society, but even the longest-range contemporary foot-commuters would fade in comparison with Jacob and Isidore Gartner, whose feet were their place of business. This father-and-son team trod country roads between Hancock and Copper Harbor, Michigan, in the hopes that folks along the way needed some piece goods, a bit of ribbon or such, as often as not receiving only coffee and conversation for their efforts. But, discouragement was too long a word to fit into their new English vocabularies, and more than a century later, their dedicated plodding is still paying dividends.

Jacob and Isidore came to America in the 1880s, arriving at Ellis Island after a particularly stormy voyage in the steerage compartment of a creaky old ship. Jacob's wife Cecilia and three additional children remained behind in Breslau, Germany, to await his return with enough money for their passage to America. The two new immigrants popped in on relatives in Detroit, Michigan, for guidance, but were told to seek their fortunes elsewhere, so, outfitting Isidore with some merchandise and a battered old suitcase, they pointed him north. He worked his way up to Sault Ste. Marie, Michigan, but he was told that the really good action was to be found in the Copper Country. Using his last coin, he wired his father to meet him there. What spunk! A teenager by himself, in a strange country with unfamiliar language, long roads, short funds, a few dollars' worth of dry goods between him and an empty belly, and a two-week walk to the Copper Country rendezvous with his father!

The walking continued long after Jacob arrived in Hancock, for Jacob's fear of horses left him no other option as they went from community to community and every farmhouse in between. They invariably received the warmest recep-tion in the most remote households, for their suitcases were the only dry goods store many of the families ever saw, and it was pretty exciting when Jacob or Isidore first raised the lid. Regardless of sales, the Gartners were frequently invited for supper and the night, partially because of their hosts' concern for their welfare, but mostly because they were reluctant to say goodbye to their first visitors in weeks. As the Gartners gained better control of both the English and Finnish languages, sales-manship improved and evening conversa-tions often extended far into the night.

During their first years in the Copper Country, the two Gartner peddlers had neither time nor money to put any frills in their living, for every dollar they saved brought them closer to their ultimate goal of a store where customers would come to them for a change. Of neces-sity, Jacob became a master of thrift and frequently their supper consisted of the free food that every saloon served with a glass of beer—two beers meant a sandwich for each and a few extra coins in the sock for their business.

When they opened their first store in 1886 on the corner of Tezcuco and Hancock Streets, their working capital was less than skimpy and if it hadn't been for the compassion of the local railway express agent, they might have gone under before their feet were even wet. All of their merchandise had to be purchased C.O.D. from Chicago, Illinois, and Milwaukee, Wisconsin, and after Jacob paid for as much of the shipment as they could afford, the agent would keep the rest in the back room until new store sales could cover the remainder of the shipping charges. Folks looked after their own in those days. After the success of the store was assured,

During their first years in the Copper Country, the two Gartner peddlers had neither time nor money to put any frills in their living, for every dollar they saved brought them closer to their ultimate goal of a store where customers would come to them for a change.

Jacob Gartner, center (in vest), and others in front of store.

Jacob's wife and children Leo, Freda, and Lucie joined their Hancock bread-winners and assisted them in the operation of a newer, bigger store they rented on Quincy Street. Although he had no schedule for the future, Jacob dreamed of a big department store in the city and laid the foundation for such a move by purchasing corner property in downtown Detroit.

After buying the Quincy Street store and adding a wing for their expanding business, prosperity was finally assured, and as the family's attachment for Hancock deepened, all thoughts of the big city disappeared. Jacob sold his Detroit property and it was just as well, for the J. L. Hudson store, which appeared on the opposite corner, would have been pretty tough competition. In the years that followed, it's likely that Jacob had occasion to ponder the wisdom of selling that corner before its potential began to surface, but he never had any regrets about staying in Hancock.

There was never any question about the Gartner children's careers, for as soon as Isidore's brother Leo and sisters Freda and Lucie could be of help, they joined the family business. Leo eventually opened his own store in Calumet, Michigan, but when a fire erased his efforts, he moved to Detroit. Freda's husband, Eugene Wollstein, managed Gartners' furniture department when it first opened and Lucie's husband, Hugo Fields, opened the Stern and Fields men's store in the west wing of Gartners'. During a 1928 trip to Germany to visit his sister, Fields met 16-year-old Norbert Kahn, a friend of his nephew, and he persuaded him to come to America

and work in his store. As soon as Norbert gained citizenship in 1933, he returned to Germany to get his sister. As the Nazi regime gained momentum, he accelerated efforts to bring more of his family to America. By the time the emigration door was slammed shut in late 1934, Norbert had personally sponsored and financed 39 relatives' moves to this country.

Norbert married Isadore's daughter Jean, and Ted Reiss, one of those he saved from the Holocaust, married her sister. When Isidore died, he left the store to his two daughters, and their husbands managed the store together. After Ted moved to Marquette, Michigan, to operate a large furniture store and Norbert had passed away, his son Richard Kahn became heir apparent to a business that began with a cardboard suitcase and a sturdy pair of shoes. The store remained in the family for over a century. Even an optimist like Jacob Gartner would never have predicted such longevity.

[Eds. notes: Jacob Gartner was born about 1843 and died December 15, 1911, in Hancock. The Gartners resided at several addresses downtown before moving to 218 Harris Avenue.]

Temple Jacob
by Susan Burack

Temple Jacob is the oldest Jewish house of worship in the Upper Peninsula. It is named for Jacob Gartner, a prominent Hancock businessman who helped found it, contributed generously to its building, and died shortly before its dedication. His descendents are members to this day.

The building was dedicated on September 1, 1912. The land was acquired in 1910 from the Quincy Mining Company. The building cornerstone bears an inscription in memory of Jacob.

Located prominently at the north end of the Portage Lake Lift Bridge, architect Charles Maass chose impressive building materials: glazed brick, native Jacobsville sandstone, and a domed, copper-colored roof adorned with the Star of David. It is, indeed, a dramatic statement for the Keweenaw.

The Hebrew inscription over the doorway reads "Congregation of Israel," which is the synagogue's state-chartered name. On the right side of the door frame is a *mezuzah* (piece of parchment), similar to those found on the doorposts of most Jewish homes. Above the entrance is a glass panel depicting a *menorah* (seven-branched lamp).

There are three doorways upon entering the building: the left leads up to a balcony; the sanctuary is straight ahead; and, the right leads down to the social room, kitchen, and restrooms. The lower-level social room was completed in the late 1940s and was recently redone.

The stained glass windows depict a series of Jewish symbols: a dove bearing an olive branch; a triangle; the tablets of the Ten Commandments; a well; the Star of David; hands in a priestly blessing; Noah's ark; the burning bush; and, a *shofar* (ram's horn).

The sanctuary is a 40-by-40 foot square. At the east side is a *bimah* (raised platform) with a reader's desk. Above it hangs the Eternal Light. The tree embroidered on the curtain behind the bimah represents the five books of Moses, or the Torah. Behind the curtain is the ark holding the Torah scrolls. Above the curtain, crouching on the ark, are two carved lions of Judah.

All of the Torah scrolls, written in ancient Hebrew, contain exactly the same words originally written down more than 3,000 years ago. The scrolls are the five books of the Hebrew Bible.

Temple Jacob celebrated its 100th anniversary with a gala weekend in August, 2012, attended by nearly 100 people from across the U.S. and as far away as Australia. The only active synagogue in Michigan on the National Register of Historic Places, Temple Jacob has a small local membership today with many long-distance supporters.

Hancock Residents in the Michigan Legislature

by John S. Haeussler,
Rob Roy, and Don Roy

How many Hancock residents have served in the Michigan Legislature? A couple? A handful? More? The answer to date is 13. A chronological introduction to each follows, with an extended overview on the first (Elijah S. Northrup) and the longest-serving (Leo H. Roy). All maintained a permanent residence in Hancock while serving in Lansing.

Elijah S. Northrup (1863)
Elijah S. Northrup is possibly Hancock's first elected official, period. He was among the initial officers, serving as clerk, when Hancock Township was organized from Portage Township in 1861. Then, prior to the initial election of village officers on March 10, 1863, Northrup was tabbed to represent the Upper Peninsula as a state senator in the 22nd Legislature, 1863-1864. A Democrat, he represented the 32nd District then consisting of Chippewa, Delta, Houghton, Keweenaw, Mackinac, Manitou, Marquette, Menominee, Ontonagon, and Schoolcraft counties including the islands and territory attached, and the islands of Lake Michigan including Green Bay, Lake Superior, the River St. Mary's, and the Straits of Mackinaw.

The 1863 legislative session began on January 7th, and Northrup was named chair of the committee on Mines and Minerals. It was a tense time, the effects of a country at war being felt everywhere. *The New York Times* reported on January 8th:

"The Michigan Legislature assembled at Lansing yesterday. The Governor's message was delivered today. Financial affairs are represented to be in a most satisfactory condition. Adequate sinking fund has been provided for the gradual extinguishment of the present state debt, and a system of taxation, not burdensome, inaugurated, which will prevent a further increase of the debt. The state has furnished altogether 45,500 soldiers, of which 24,200 were sent to the field previous to July last. Two thousand are yet to be raised to fill the quota under the last call. Alluding to the Proclamation of Emancipation, which is heartily indorsed, he says: 'We are about to shake hands with the entire loyal population of the South, whether white or black. We shall no longer respect the claim of a white traitor to compel a black loyalist to aid him in destroying the government.'"

Less than two months later, on March 2nd, Elijah S. Northrup was dead.

On March 4th, Senator Andrew S. Robertson, a lawyer from Mt. Clemens, addressed the Senate:

"Mr. President—It is my painful duty now to announce to this Senate the death of the senator from the 32nd District, Hon. E. S. Northrup, who departed this life on Monday night, after a lingering illness. He had long been the doomed victim of consumption, and had found safety and health, for the last few years, in the pure air of the Lake Superior country. Elected as their senator, by a generous and confiding constituency, he periled his life for them, by repairing to and remaining at his post of duty, at this capital, during this inclement winter. He has fallen! But, his memory will long be held sacred by his constituency, as it will long be cherished by us.

To us, this is indeed an affliction and a solemn warning. It is not often that the Fell Destroyer has entered this chamber—I do not know if ever before. The fact should, therefore, give rise to the most serious reflections; for it has pleased God to bring the nothingness of man, and the vanity of his petty ambitions, terribly near to us. Senator Northrup was comparatively a young man, just 34 years of age, in the prime of his manhood, and with a fair career of usefulness before him. He had endeared himself to the Senate by his gentle courtesy, his manly sentiments, his scorn of all mere shams, his undoubted patriotism, and his devotion to business. We mourn his loss; but, we mourn not without hope. That vacant chair may be—will be—filled by an estimable and worthy man, and the place that once knew him will know our friend no more forever. The State will have the services of another patriotic son, and he shall be forgotten. But who shall dry the tears of his orphaned children, or assuage the grief of his mourning widow? It is of this the minstrel sings:

"Tis night and the landscape is lovely no more, I mourn, but ye woodlands! I mourn not for you! For morn shall return, your charms to restore, perfumed with fresh fragrance and glittering with dew. Nor yet for the ravage of winter I mourn,—kind nature the embryo blossom will save; but when shall spring visit the mouldering urn? Oh! When shall day dawn on the night of the grave?'

May that Good Shepherd, who can temper the winds to the shorn lamb, sustain them in His sheltering arms, in this the hour of their trial.

Mr. President, as expressive of the respect of this body, I move the adoption of the following resolutions:

It having pleased God to remove from among us, our most respected colleague, Elijah S. Northrup, senator from the 32nd District, in the midst of a career of usefulness, at an early age, and after his having, during the brief period of our intercourse, endeared himself to us, by his gentle courtesy and unvarying urbanity;

Resolved, by the Senate of the State of Michigan, that we recognize, in this afflictive stroke, the hand of Him who turns to nought the counsels of the wise, yet doeth all things well; that we deeply sympathize with his bereaved wife and family, and tender to them our sincerest condolence—ourselves grieving that all we can do cannot assuage the sorrow, nor dry the tears, of those so near and dear.

Resolved, that a committee of three, on the part of the Senate, be appointed, to act in conjunction with a committee of the House, to arrange for the celebration of his obsequies, in an appropriate manner.

Resolved, that in respect to the memory of our departed colleague, the members of this body will wear the usual badge of mourning, for 30 days; and, as a further mark of respect, that the Senate do now adjourn.

Resolved, that a duly certified copy of these resolutions, be presented to the widow of the deceased."

Also on March 4th, following an announcement to the House of Senator Northrup's death, Representative John Q. McKernan, a millwright from Houghton, Michigan, and fellow New Yorker by birth, addressed the House:

"Mr. Speaker—The above communication announces to this House the sudden death of the Hon. Elijah S. Northrup, senator from the 32nd District, who departed this life on the 2nd instant, at his lodgings in this city, after a lingering sickness.

As a member from the Upper Peninsula, it becomes my painful duty to offer the following resolutions as a tribute of respect to his memory.

Mr. Northrup was born in the town of Stafford, Genesee County, in the State of New York, in the year 1829. He lived in that county until the year 1850, when he removed to Saline, in Washtenaw County, in this state, and there engaged in mercantile business. He has been a resident of Houghton County since 1861, where he has been engaged in business as insurance agent and enjoyed an exalted reputation for probity and justice. During that time I have been somewhat acquainted with him, both in business relations and as a neighbor. He was a high-minded man, kind-hearted, and possessed social qualities, which made him numerous friends. To be acquainted with him was to honor and respect him. He never turned a deaf ear to the appeals of sorrow or suffering, but to the extent of his ability, he was ever ready to aid, comfort, and console.

He enjoyed the confidence and respect of all who knew him, as is evident from the fact that he held several offices of honor and trust at the same time.

But, alas! Like many others, he has fallen in the time of his greatest usefulness. He has, unfortunately, performed his last and solemn duty as a public officer, and our rich mineral district, which he represented, is now without a senator, and his duties will now devolve on other men.

His death is an irreparable loss to the Upper Peninsula, and his constituents and friends will have much reason to mourn his loss—cut down in the prime of life—permanently withdrawn from this world, by an All-Wise Providence, whose ways are inscrutable, and whose call we must obey. In the midst of life, we are in death. Sooner or later, we must all follow him to that home whence no traveler returns.

Mr. Speaker, I offer the following resolutions:

Whereas, it has pleased a Divine Providence to remove from our midst, the Hon. Elijah S. Northrup, senator from the 32nd Senatorial District, whilst actively engaged in his senatorial duties, at the capitol of the state;

And whereas, this melancholy event has cast a deep gloom over the action of this Legislature, and deprived the state of one of its ablest members, his constituents of a faithful advocate, and his family of a worthy protector;

And whereas, it is deemed proper that on this sad occasion we should pay a just tribute of respect and affection to an honored and faithful legislator; therefore,

Be it resolved, that the members and officers of this House wear the usual badge of mourning during the session.

Resolved, that we tender to the family of the deceased our heartfelt sympathies and condolence in this the hour of their sad affliction and bereavement.

Resolved, that in token of our esteem for the lamented deceased, this House do attend the funeral services, in a body.

Resolved, that the clerk of this House be and is hereby instructed to transmit a copy of these resolutions to the family of the deceased.

Resolved, that in respect to the memory of the departed, the House do now adjourn."

Senator Northrup was not replaced in the 1863-1864 Legislature. He was succeeded by John H. Forster, of Houghton, in 1865.

Charles E. Holland (1871-1872)

Charles E. Holland was born on June 30, 1835, in Indianapolis, Indiana. He moved to Ontonagon, Michigan, in 1853, and lived there for five years before returning to Indianapolis. He settled in Hancock in 1862. Holland was a merchant and actively engaged in developing the resources of the Upper Peninsula. He was a co-lessee (with Joseph H. Chandler, among others) in 1869 of the Albany & Boston Mining Company in Houghton and operated it briefly at a substantial loss. He was Hancock village president from 1868 to 1871. A Republican, Holland was elected as representative of Houghton County in the 1871-1872 State Legislature. He served on the Internal Improvements, Mines and Minerals, and State Affairs committees. The 1871 legislative session ended on April 18th, allowing Holland to turn his attention to the Mineral Range Railroad Company, organized on June 19th, for which he served as president. Holland was an original incorporator of the Merchants' & Miners' Bank in Calumet, Michigan, in July, 1873, and an organizer and director of the First National Bank of Hancock, established in 1874. He left Hancock in 1886, retiring to Detroit, Michigan, where he died on October 25, 1891.

Seth D. North (1877-1886)

Seth D. North was born on April 9, 1823, in Middlesex County, Connecticut. He received his education and started his family there before moving to Ontonagon in the late 1850s. He was a warehouse clerk in Ontonagon, and then in Rockland, Michigan, where he later established a general store. North purchased the Quincy Mining Company store in Hancock in September, 1866, and resided at the mine thereafter. North ran the Quincy store, previously operated by the company at a loss, as a profitable venture for several decades. A popular Republican, North represented Houghton County in the State House in 1877-1878 and 1881-1886. He represented the 32nd District comprised of Houghton, Isle Royal, Keweenaw, and Ontonagon counties in the State Senate in 1879-1880. His ten years of service in the Michigan Legislature established a record for Hancock residents equaled only by Leo H. Roy. His committee assignments included the Geological Survey; Harbors; Immigration; Michigan Institution for the Deaf and Dumb; Mines and Minerals, and Mining Interests; Municipal Corporations; Private Corporations; Roads and Bridges; Rules and Joint Rules; State House of Correction; and University committees. North was an organizer and president of the First National Bank of Hancock and a director of the Mineral Range Railroad Company and Sturgeon River Lumber Company. Seth D. North died in 1893, and his son, George S., continued operation of the Quincy store for many years to follow.

Joseph H. Chandler (1881-1882)

Joseph H. Chandler was born in Niles, Cayuga County, New York, on July 30, 1842. He moved to Michigan in 1857, residing in Washtenaw County until 1868. Chandler entered the U.S. Army in 1862, serving until 1866. He was a charter member of the Edmund R. Stiles Grand Army of the Republic Post No. 174 in Hancock. He was admitted to the bar in 1869 in Houghton County and, in the 1870s, he had a private law practice with Claudius Grant, a future Michigan Supreme Court justice. Chandler briefly operated the Albany & Boston Mining Company and was an organizer of the First National Bank of Hancock, partnering with Charles E. Holland and others in both ventures. He also served as prosecuting attorney for Houghton County and collector of customs for the District of Superior. Chandler succeeded Seth D. North as state senator from the 32nd District in 1881-1882. A Republican, he ran unopposed and was supported by both major parties. He served on the Insurance; Mines, Minerals, and Mining Interests; Public Lands; and, Railroads committees. Chandler left Hancock later in the 1880s for Chicago, Illinois.

Thomas B. Dunstan (1889-1890)
Thomas Bree Dunstan was born on January 4, 1850, in Camborne, Cornwall County, England. His family immigrated in 1854, settling in Ontonagon County, Michigan. Dunstan graduated from Lawrence University, Appleton, Wisconsin, in 1871, and he entered the University of Michigan Law School. Following his admittance to the bar, he was elected judge of probate and prosecuting attorney for Keweenaw County in November, 1872. He held those offices through July, 1879, when he moved to Pontiac, Michigan. He returned to Keweenaw County's Central Mine in 1882, and he was elected to represent the Keweenaw District in the State House. He moved to Hancock in 1883, and he was elected prosecuting attorney for Houghton County the following year. A Republican, Dunstan was again nominated for the office of prosecuting attorney in 1886, and he was endorsed by both the Republican and Democratic parties. He was a Michigan delegate-at-large

to the Republican National Convention in 1888. He was elected state senator from the 32nd District, then comprising the counties of Baraga, Houghton, Isle Royal, Keweenaw, and Ontonagon, for 1889-1890. He served on the Asylum for the Criminal Insane, Executive Business, Immigration, Judiciary, Mining School and Mining Interests, and Reformatory at Ionia committees. Dunstan was appointed to the Board of Control of the Michigan College of Mines (now Michigan Technological University) by Governor John T. Rich. He was also a director of the Adventure Consolidated Copper Company, First National Bank of Hancock, Quincy & Torch Lake Railroad Company, and Rhode Island Mining Company, president of the Ontonagon County National Bank and Victoria Copper Mining Company, and counsel to the Quincy Mining Company. Dunstan was elected lieutenant governor of Michigan for 1897-1898, the highest position in Michigan State office attained by a Hancock resident. As lieutenant governor he received a salary of $3.00 per day while the Legislature was in session. He was a trustee of Lawrence University from 1899 to 1902 and resided at 305 Water Street. Thomas Bree Dunstan died at the Auditorium Building in Chicago, May 23, 1902, a result of a complication of diseases. He is buried in Hancock's Lakeside Cemetery and Dunstan Street is named in his honor.

Harry C. Southworth (1889-1890)
Harry C. Southworth was born in Stoughton, Massachusetts, on February 26, 1857. He moved to Houghton County in 1877, following his graduation from the Massachusetts Institute of Technology. He worked in the mills of the Quincy Mining Company as an assayer. A Republican, Southworth was elected to represent Houghton County in the Michigan House of Representatives in 1889-1890, concurrent with Thomas B. Dunstan's term as a senator. He served

on the Geological Survey and School of Mines committees. Southworth returned to his native Stoughton in the 1890s and remained active in community affairs.

William Harry (1891-1892)

William Harry was born on August 14, 1842, in Cornwall, England. Orphaned at age 12, he continued his education while working and saved enough of his earnings to secure passage to America at age 19. He first engaged as a timekeeper in an iron mine near Dover, New Jersey. He moved to Hancock in 1863, working in the copper mines prior to learning the tinsmith's trade. In 1869, he opened his own tin, sheet iron, copper, and hardware business at 116 Quincy Street. Harry organized the Hancock Banking Company, served as a director and president of the First National Bank of Hancock, and was prominently connected with the Northern Michigan Building and Loan Association and the Peninsular Electric Light Company. He was also elected to serve as one of Hancock's first fire wardens. Preferring to focus his time and efforts on his business interests, Harry did not enter the political arena until retiring from active mercantile life in 1890. A Republican, he was elected to the 1891-1892 State Legislature as representative of Houghton County, succeeding Harry C. Southworth. He served on the Federal Relations and Mines and Minerals committees. William Harry resided at 211 Hancock Street prior to moving to Detroit in 1900. He died there on April 20, 1914.

George W. Rulison (1897-1902)

George W. Rulison was born on March 7, 1834, in Watertown, Jefferson County, New York. He was born on a farm and lived there until the age of 17. Commencing in 1855, he spent two years in Wisconsin, two in Minnesota, one in Kansas, a few in the gold-mining industry in Colorado, and eventually returned to Wisconsin to become a school teacher. He moved to Houghton County in 1866, and he found employment as a teacher, a clerk for a lumber and mill yard, and in real estate. He was active in the community, holding the following offices at various times: county clerk, justice of the peace, school inspector, township supervisor, and village trustee. A Republican, Rulison represented Houghton County's 2nd District in the State House from 1897 to 1902. The 2nd District comprised the townships of Adams, Chassell, Duncan, Franklin, Hancock, Laird, Osceola, Portage, and Quincy. He served on the Education, Game Laws, Institution for the Deaf and Dumb, Local Taxation, Public Health, Railroads, School for the Deaf, State Library, and Ways and Means committees. Rulison resided in the Pewabic House, 222 Hancock Street, in the early 1880s, and later at 605 Hancock Street. George W. Rulison died of heart disease in Hancock, August 24, 1903. He is buried in Hancock's Lakeside Cemetery.

Alvin D. Pettit (1903-1906)

Alvin D. Pettit was born in Emerson Township, Gratiot County, Michigan, on December 6, 1856. He was orphaned at age ten and spent the next five years working on farms in the summer and attending school in Ithaca, Michigan, in the winter. He began work in a printing office at age 15 and, save for serving as Ithaca's postmaster from 1891 to 1895, remained in the printing profession throughout his career. He was active with the Republican Party in both Gratiot and Houghton counties, and he represented the newly-formed 3rd District of Houghton County in the Michigan House of Representatives from 1903 to 1906. In Pettit's first term the 3rd District contained the townships of Adams, Chassell, Duncan, Elm River, Hancock, Laird, Portage, and Quincy. The City of Hancock and Stanton Township were recognized as part of the district for the 1905-1906 session. Pettit served on the Labor, Normal Schools, Printing, and Public Health committees. Bucking the trend among Upper Peninsula representatives to be a conservative corporationist, Pettit supported liberal reform policies including rigid regulation of corporations. This prompted Rep. William J. Galbraith of Calumet Township to state, "I wish to heavens Pettit would go back to the Lower Peninsula where he came from. He's no good to us." Upon returning to Hancock, Alvin D. Pettit briefly resided at 313 Dakota Street. Little else is known about him following his service in Lansing. Perhaps Galbraith's wish was granted.

W. Frank James (1911-1914)
William Francis James was born on May 23, 1873, in Morristown, New Jersey. In 1876, his family moved to Hancock, where he was educated in the public schools prior to attending Albion College. He served as a private in Company F of the 34th Regiment, Michigan Volunteer Infantry, during the Spanish-American War. Following the war he became engaged in insurance and real estate. He was Houghton County treasurer from 1901 to 1904, and mayor of Hancock from 1909 to 1911. A Republican, James was elected to the State Senate from the 32nd District of Baraga, Houghton, Keweenaw, and Ontonagon counties for 1911-1914. He served on the Apportionment, Asylum for Insane at Newberry, Cities and Villages, College of Mines, Elections, Geological Survey, Ionia State Hospital, Labor Interests, State Asylum, and Taxation committees. Following his tenure in the Michigan Senate, James served ten consecutive terms, 1915-1934, in the U.S. Congress as the representative from Michigan's 12th District of Baraga, Dickinson, Gogebic, Houghton, Iron, Keweenaw, Marquette, and Ontonagon counties. His national service included chairing the Committee on Military Affairs in 1929-1930. He resided at 1318 Emery Street. W. Frank James died in Arlington, Virginia, November 17, 1945. He is buried at the Arlington National Cemetery.

Leo H. Roy (1949-1958)
"Get on your mark. Get ready. Get set. Go!" These words were spoken by the starter at the Michigan College of Mines Winter Carnival speed skating contest held in Houghton's Amphidrome on February 23, 1923. Leo "Dago" Roy, a ninth-grade student at Houghton High School, was a participant. Leo won that race, but eligibility rules

kept him from accepting the prize. Little did he know that it would be one of many races to come. Dago's only objective was to win. This winning attitude and competitive spirit continued throughout his life. The Roy family was part of a wave of French-Canadian immigrants that came to the Upper Peninsula of Michigan in the 1800s. Leo's grandparents, Francois and Sophia (Robarge) Roy, emigrated from Lacolle, Quebec, Canada, to Lake Linden, Michigan, in 1879. Francois helped establish the Poull Mercantile Company in Lake Linden. He also served as treasurer of the village and of the building fund for St. Joseph's Church.

The Roy family had seven children including son Emile, born on August 9, 1876, in Lacolle. Emile married Mary Louise Brule of Lake Linden on July 15, 1903. They moved to Houghton in 1906, and they had seven children of their own. Emile managed the circulation department of *The Daily Mining Gazette* for 21 years, and he was a salesman for Roach and Seeber Wholesale in Houghton until his death on April 25, 1925.

Leo Homer Roy was the third child of Emile and Mary Louise, born on May 6, 1908. He was 16 at the time of his father's death and became a bread-winner for the family. Leo delivered papers and drove a bakery wagon. The other Roy brothers also helped support the family, and Mary Louise took in boarders to cover expenses.

Like most young boys, Leo was involved with his brothers in neighborhood sports. He excelled at football and hockey in high school, the latter having the biggest influence on his future. During his senior year, Leo was recruited to play semi-pro hockey with the Radio Six team from Hurontown, Michigan. His performance caught the attention of the Portage Lake club, which

he joined later during the 1925-26 season. He was recruited by Michigan College of Mines coach Carlos "Cub" Haug for 1926-27. Leo spent two years in college, playing football and hockey, before leaving to enter the insurance field.

He learned the insurance trade at Southern Surety in St. Louis, Missouri. Upon returning to the Copper Country, he was employed by the N. J. Brodeur Insurance Agency in Hancock.

Leo married Dorothy MacDonald from Ontonagon at Hancock's St. Patrick's Church on August 30, 1932. They raised three children: Robert (Rob), Dorothy, and Donald (Don). The Roy's primary residence was 202 Harris Avenue.

In the summer of 1933, Leo left the Brodeur Agency and, with his wife, opened the Leo H. Roy Insurance Agency at 412 Quincy Street. The agency later moved to 101-103 Quincy Street and operated in Hancock for 50 years until its sale in 1983. During the early years, Leo was active with many local organizations. He remained involved with hockey, managing and coaching the Hancock Bears semi-pro team and refereeing in the Michigan-Wisconsin Senior League. As his business succeeded, Leo became less involved with hockey and more active in community affairs and service functions.

Leo's competitive side resurfaced in 1948 when he decided to run for the Michigan State Senate. A Republican, he was elected to represent the 32nd District. Leo joined the Senate in January, 1949, and had a successful tenure in the Michigan Legislature through 1958. He was elected to five consecutive two-year terms, thereby equaling the record established by Seth D. North for longest tenure in the State Legislature by a Hancock resident.

One of Leo's first campaign promises was to obtain funds for the construction of the Copper Country Tuberculosis Sanatorium (now the Houghton County Medical Care Facility) in Hancock. His work on this project was successful and over the next ten years he headed several projects that benefited the district. Leo felt that one had to "get along" with both sides and be willing to compromise, and this attitude contributed to his success in the Senate.

In the early 1950s, Michigan Tech President Grover C. Dillman formulated plans to change the face of the school. He approached Senator Roy for support and together they developed a future campus plan, which was continued when Dr. Robert Van Pelt succeeded Dillman. Through the cooperation of Senator Roy and the Michigan Legislature, funds were appropriated for the Civil Geology Building, Ores Research Laboratory, Fisher Hall, and the Mathematics and Physics Building. Leo's biggest battle occurred during the 1953 session when funds were requested for an artificial ice plant in Dee Stadium, then home to the Michigan Tech hockey team. After a number of heated arguments in the Senate, the funds were allocated by eight votes.

Senator Roy's service also included membership on the Appropriations, Banks and Corporations, Conservation, Highways, Insurance (for which he served as chairman), State Affairs, and Veterans' Affairs committees. He proposed and realized funding for the Mackinac Bridge, and he played a pivotal role in the development of the Portage Lake Lift Bridge; the expansion of the highway from Ontonagon to Watersmeet, Michigan; the development of the *Ranger III*; and, the expansion of Baraga, Fort Wilkins, McLain, and Porcupine Mountains state parks, and the Isle Royale National Park. He

proposed legislation for snow-removal funding, insurance revisions, increased worker's compensation, aid to dairy and agriculture industries, and renovation of the Sturgeon River flowage areas. Senator Roy obtained funding for the renovations to the Calumet Armory and served on the Governor's Advisory Commission on Reorganization of State Government.

Leo was active in the Copper Country community organizing the Hancock Lions Club, chairing the Houghton County Price and Rationing Board, and serving as president of the Hancock Board of Education, Hancock Chamber of Commerce, and Portage Lake Chamber of Commerce. He was a member of several other local service and social organizations.

"I remember him as being an honest and sincere gentleman," remarked his son, Don. "Treat everybody with honesty. That's what I learned from him." A man who served his family, community, state, and team, Leo H. Roy died in Chassell, Michigan, on September 11, 1968.

Stephen P. Dresch (1991-1992)

Stephen P. Dresch was born in East St. Louis, Illinois, on December 12, 1943. He received an A.B. in Philosophy from Miami University (Ohio), 1963, M.Phil. in Economics from Yale University, 1966, and Ph.D. in Economics from Yale, 1970. He enjoyed a distinguished and well-traveled career as an economist. Among his many positions, he was a research associate at the National Bureau of Economic Research; taught at Southern Connecticut State College, Rutgers University, and Yale University; was a research scholar at the International Institute for Applied Systems Analysis, Austria; and, was a visiting scholar at the Institute of Economics and Forecasting of Scientific and Technological Progress, U.S.S.R. Academy of Sciences. Dresch arrived in the Copper Country in 1985 as dean of Michigan Technological University's School of Business and Engineering Administration. His five-year tenure was focused on exposing significant financial malfeasance among the school's administration, ending in the closing of a corrupt economic venture and the beginning of a political career. A libertarian Republican, Dresch was elected to represent the 110th District of Gogebic, Houghton, Iron, Keweenaw, and Ontonagon counties in the 1991-1992 State House. He served on the Civil Rights, Constitution and Women's Issues, Marine Affairs and Port Development, Social Services and Youth, and Transportation committees. Describing the Legislature as "an inbred, self-serving political establishment," Dresch sought to expose corruption, incompetence, and negligence whenever and wherever he encountered it. Following his term in office, Dresch continued as an independent political activist and critic, and became an expert witness in administrative, legislative, and juridical proceedings. He operated Forensic Intelligence International from his home at 318 Cooper Avenue, and he was involved in multiple high-profile national cases as an independent investigator. Stephen P. Dresch died of lung cancer at his home in Hancock on August 6, 2006. His widow, Linda Dresch, continues to reside at 318 Cooper Avenue.

Michael A. Lahti (2007-2010)

Michael A. Lahti was born on October 10, 1945, in Highland Park, Michigan, where his parents had moved temporarily during World War II. He returned to Hancock as an infant, and he is a graduate of the Hancock Public Schools and Northern Michigan University. His father, Leonard Lahti, was Hancock's mayor from 1954 to 1961. In 1966, Mike married fellow Hancock native Sharon Pardini. They have four daughters and two sons. Lahti has operated the State Farm Insurance agency in Hancock for over 40 years. He is also a prominent land owner and real estate developer in the Western Upper Peninsula. In this capacity, Lahti is responsible for much of the historic preservation and rehabilitation that has recently been completed throughout the Copper Country. He served on the Hancock Board of Education for seven years, chaired the Houghton County Board of Commissioners for six years, and is a member of the Finlandia University Board of Trustees, a position he's held in excess of 15 years. He was elected to represent the 110th District of Baraga, Gogebic, Houghton, Iron, Keweenaw, Ontonagon, and part of Marquette counties in the Michigan House of Representatives from 2007 to 2010. He was the first Democrat from Hancock in the State Legislature since Elijah S. Northrup in 1863. A member of the Appropriations Committee, he chaired the Natural Resources and Environment subcommittee and served on the Corrections, General Government, Human Services, and Joint Capital Outlay subcommittees. Among his significant accomplishments during his two terms in office, Lahti was able to save the Calumet State Police Post and procure funding for Michigan Tech's Great Lakes Research Center. Rep. Steve Lindberg, of the 109th District, says, "Mike Lahti is an intelligent man who approaches life from a practical, common sense point of view. In the four years I served with him in the House of Representatives, no one in the Legislature worked harder in their district or in Lansing than Mike. Combined with his high sense of ethics, this makes Mike Lahti's career one that is recognized for serving the 110th District with the highest distinction." Michael A. and Sharon Lahti reside at 913 Quincy Street.

Verna Hillie

Hancock's claim to film fame is attributed to Verna Hillie. Born May 5, 1914, in Hancock, Verna is the daughter of Edward W. and Lempi K. Hillie.[1] The family resided at 816 Franklin Street and Edward was employed as a bookkeeper at the Quincy Smelter.

HANCOCK 1863 - 2013

by Roland Burgan

The Hillies relocated to Detroit, Michigan, during Verna's childhood. There she began performing in radio dramas, immensely popular in that era, which made her a local celebrity by her teenage years.

Verna was one of four finalists in a Paramount Pictures nationwide talent search in 1931. The winner received a role in an upcoming film and, although Verna wasn't chosen for this part, she did catch the eye of a director as a promising talent. Her Hollywood debut was a brief appearance in 1932's *Madame Butterfly*, which starred Cary Grant. She was 18 at the time.

By 1933, Verna was being cast as the female lead opposite other rising stars. Her first major part was in the Zane Grey western, *Man of the Forest*, with Randolph Scott. Verna's next leading role was in the 1934 horror-mystery, *House of Mystery*. She got back in the saddle starring with John Wayne in a pair of 1934 westerns, *The Star Packer* and *The Trail Beyond*. Verna continued her most productive film year with the lead in another western, *Mystery Mountain*, with Ken Maynard.

Verna appeared in three more movies in 1935 before relocating to New York. She had married Frank Gill, Jr., a radio performer and scriptwriter, in 1933, and both had opportunities in the Big Apple. Verna appeared in the 1935-1936 Broadway production of the Ayn Rand play *Night of*

January 16th and Frank wrote for the radio networks, which had an emerging national audience.

Verna twice returned to Hollywood for additional movie roles. She co-starred with Marjorie Reynolds and Sheila Bromley in the 1938 drama, *Rebellious Daughters*, and appeared in the 1941 Disney film, *The Reluctant Dragon*.

Following a career of at least 18 appearances, Verna retired from the movie business and devoted her time to raising her two daughters, Pamela and Kelly. Pamela (Lincoln) had an acting career of her own, including an appearance in the popular 1982 film, *Tootsie*. Verna and Frank divorced in 1952, and she was later married to writer Richard Linkroum for a short time.

Verna was briefly back in show business in the early 1950s, making multiple television appearances on the *George Burns and Gracie Allen Show*. She later became the U.S. representative for writer Dame Barbara Cartland, whose books sold roughly one billion copies in the 20th century.

After spending most of her adult life in New York, Verna Hillie died in Fairfax, Connecticut, on October 3, 1997. She is Hancock's most recognizable performer from the Golden Age of Hollywood.

Verna Hillie

The following is a list of films in which Verna Hillie appeared and some of the stars with whom she performed:

Madame Butterfly (1932) Cary Grant, Sylvia Sydney, and Charles Ruggles

From Hell to Heaven (1933) Carole Lombard and Jack Oakie

Under the Tonto Rim (1933) Stuart Erwin

Man of the Forest (1933) Randolph Scott, Harry Carey, Noah Beery, Barton MacLane, and Buster Crabbe

Duck Soup (1933) The Marx Brothers

Search for Beauty (1934) Buster Crabbe, Ida Lupino, Robert Armstrong, and James Gleason

Six of a Kind (1934) Charles Ruggles, W. C. Fields, George Burns, and Gracie Allen

House of Mystery (1934) Gabby Hayes

The Star Packer (1934) John Wayne, Gabby Hayes, and Yakima Canutt

Romance in the Rain (1934) Roger Pryor

The Trail Beyond (1934) John Wayne, Noah Beery, and Noah Beery, Jr.

Mystery Mountain (1934) Ken Maynard

I've Been Around (1934) Chester Morris and Gene Lockhart

Princess O'Hara (1935) Chester Morris

Mister Dynamite (1935) Edmund Lowe

Rescue Squad (1935) Ralph Forbes and Leon Ames

Rebellious Daughters (1938) Marjorie Reynolds and Sheila Bromley

The Reluctant Dragon (1941) Robert Benchley, Frances Gifford, and Alan Ladd

Verna Hillie

[1] Edward Verner Etelamaki was born in Alavus, Finland. His name was changed to *Edward W. Hillie - etela* means *south* and *maki* means *hill* in Finnish - prior to marrying. Lempi Rasinen was born in Calumet, Michigan, to Finnish parents. As an adult, Lempi was known as *Catherine Hillie.*

By 1933, Verna was being cast as the female lead opposite other rising stars.

John Wayne and Verna Hillie in *The Star Packer*, 1934.

Harpo Marx and Verna Hillie in *Duck Soup*, 1933.

Randolph Scott, Verna Hillie, and Vince Barnett in *Man of the Forest*, 1933.

Hancock proudly claims four Olympic athletes, all of whom, fittingly, participated in winter sports.

Hancock Olympians

by Zach Hope

Rod Paavola

Rodney Earland "Rod" Paavola was born on August 21, 1939, in Hancock. A member of the 1960 U.S. Hockey Team, he was the first Olympian to hail from Hancock. In his youth, Paavola frequently played on the rink at Hancock's now-defunct Hillside Athletic Club. He was a gifted athlete on and off the ice, setting an Upper Peninsula record in the pole vault and being named to the All-U.P. Football Team while attending Hancock Central High School.

Paavola was first selected to represent the U.S. in hockey at the 1959 World Championships in Prague, Czechoslovakia, where the Americans finished fourth. He was a gritty defenseman, standing six feet tall and weighing 190 pounds. He primarily made his presence known behind his team's blue line.

Paavola was invited to try out for the 1960 Olympic Team by Coach Jack Riley due to his strong play in the World Championships. He made the team, which was picked to finish last by *Sports Illustrated*. However, the U.S. team made an improbable run in Squaw Valley, California, winning all seven of their games and capturing the U.S.'s first Olympic gold medal in hockey. The medal round featured a stunning upset of the U.S.S.R., the defending Olympic champions, 3-2. The 1960 U.S. gold medal is known now as the "Forgotten Miracle," referencing the U.S.'s 1980 "Miracle on Ice" team which also upset the Soviets en route to a gold medal.

Following the 1960 Olympic victory, Paavola fulfilled his obligation to the U.S. Army. He was drafted by the New York Rangers of the National Hockey League, and he played professionally for a handful of seasons, primarily with the International Hockey League's Muskegon Zephyrs. He coached the Portage Lake Pioneers to two Great Lakes Hockey League championships and later coached at Jeffers High School in Painesdale, Michigan. His coaching style mimicked the hard-nosed ruggedness he displayed as a player.

Paavola was inducted into the Upper Peninsula Sports Hall of Fame in 1985. The 1960 gold medal team was inducted into the U.S. Hockey Hall of Fame in 2000 and received the Lester Patrick Award in 2002 for its contribution to ice hockey in the U.S.

Rod Paavola died in Marquette, Michigan, on December 3, 1995. He is buried in Hancock's Lakeside Cemetery. Rod's Hancock childhood home was at 25 Shafter Street.

Paul Coppo

Paul "Racket" Coppo was born on November 2, 1938, in Hancock. He first showed promise as a hockey player on Hancock's Laurn-Grove rink, where he learned to skate. He was a standout player in Copper Country youth leagues and played collegiately at Michigan Technological University. Coppo led the Huskies in scoring as a sophomore in 1957-58 and again as a senior in 1959-60, when he led the team to the national championship game and garnered All-American and All-Tournament honors. A 5-foot-11, 176-pound centerman, he was lauded for his sportsmanship, receiving only six penalties during his 85-game collegiate career.

Coppo was a member of the 1964 U.S. Olympic Team that placed fifth in Innsbruck, Austria. He led the team in scoring with seven points in seven games. He also represented the United States at the 1962, 1965, 1966, and 1969 World Championships. The 1962 team won a bronze medal.

Coppo played professionally with the Green Bay Bobcats of the United States Hockey League. Beginning in 1960, he spent 15 seasons with the Bobcats including serving as coach for the final four seasons while occasionally still appearing in games. He retired as the team's all-time leading scorer with 559 points and was named an all-star six times. He later coached for eight seasons in the De Pere (Wisconsin) Youth Hockey Association, winning three Wisconsin Amateur Hockey Association state tournaments.

Coppo was inducted into the Upper Peninsula Sports Hall of Fame in 1982, the Michigan Tech Sports Hall of Fame in 1985, the U.S. Hockey Hall of Fame in 2004, and the Wisconsin Hockey Hall of Fame in 2006.

Paul Coppo resides in De Pere, Wisconsin. His Hancock childhood home was at 79 Hill Street, between 3rd and 4th Streets.

Bruce Riutta

Bruce Henry Riutta was born on October 14, 1944, in Hancock. A Copper Country legend, he led his Dollar Bay pee wee and midget hockey teams to national championships. Riutta continued his winning ways as a collegian capturing the 1965 national championship with Michigan Tech. A 6-foot-3, 196-pound defenseman, he received All-American honors for the 1965-66 and 1966-67 seasons.

Riutta represented the U.S. on the 1968 Olympic Team, which finished sixth in Grenoble, France. He remained a member of the U.S. National Team that competed in the World Championships in 1969, 1970, and 1971, winning the Group B Pool in 1970.

Riutta joined Paul Coppo on the United States Hockey League's Green Bay Bobcats team in 1968 and played professionally there through the mid-1970s. He was instrumental in the development of youth and high school hockey in Ashwaubenon, Wisconsin, where he coached and mentored for 25 years.

Riutta was inducted into the Michigan Tech Sports Hall of Fame in 1987 and the Upper Peninsula Sports Hall of Fame in 2006.

Bruce Riutta died in Houston, Texas, on January 24, 2012. His Hancock childhood home was at 933 4th Street.

Mary Seaton Brush

Mary Lon Seaton was born on July 18, 1956, in Virginia, Minnesota. She began downhill skiing at the age of four at Mont Ripley, just outside of Hancock. Seaton grew up in a family of skiers and spent much of her early winters on the slopes with her siblings and parents. At the age of five she began attending Weber's Ski School in Bay Mills, Michigan, during Christmas breaks from classes and also started skiing in family races hosted by Mont Ripley.

Seaton's formal downhill racing career began at age 11 when she joined the Copper Country Ski Club. At age 14 she joined the Hancock Central High School team and also entered events hosted by the United States Ski Association (USSA). Seaton participated in the Central Division of the USSA and stood out from the competition immediately. She won the first event she entered and regularly placed at the top of the leader board. She earned a spot on the U.S. Junior National Team and invitations to the Junior Olympics from 1973 to 1975. Seaton was named the top female skier in the USSA Central Division in 1974.

At Hancock Central High School, Seaton was awarded first team all-state and team most valuable player in each of her four seasons. She led the Bulldogs to state championships as a junior (1973) and senior (1974). In addition to skiing, Seaton excelled in other high school athletics. She was named most valuable player in both basketball and track and field as a senior. Seaton received first team all-district honors in basketball. She also competed in the Upper Peninsula Track and Field Finals, where she won the 80-yard low hurdles and placed in the high jump and long jump.

Seaton raced one year as a post-graduate student at Burke Mountain Academy, a famous ski school in East Burke, Vermont. Following a successful season at Burke, she was named to the U.S. Ski Team in the spring of 1975. She represented the U.S. at the 1976 Olympics in Innsbruck, Austria, where she finished 10th in the slalom and 17th in the giant slalom. Seaton remained on the U.S. Ski Team and competed on the World Cup circuit through 1979. She had multiple top-ten finishes in both the United States and Europe, highlighted by a second-place finish in the slalom at the 1976 U.S. National Alpine Championships.

In 1979, Seaton enrolled at the University of Vermont and joined the ski team that winter. She won all but one slalom race and placed third or better in every giant slalom race on the college circuit. Led by Seaton's national championship in slalom, Vermont placed second in the nation as a team. Combined with her slalom title, Seaton's third-place finish

in the giant slalom gave her the overall individual national championship. She was honored by *Ski Racing Magazine* as Female Collegiate Skier of the Year.

Seaton moved to the U.S. Pro Ski Tour in 1980. She finished fifth overall in 1982 and retired from competitive racing following the 1983 season.

Now Mary Seaton Brush, she resides in Charlotte, Vermont, and continues to ski every winter with her husband and their two daughters. Mary's Hancock childhood home was at 309 Harris Avenue.

NOTE: Paul Coppo, Rod Paavola, and Mary Seaton were part of the 2007 inaugural class inducted into the Hancock Central High School Athletic Hall of Fame.

The following publications contain, in full or part, historical content on Hancock. Included are publications focusing on the Quincy Mining Company.

1887-8 Hand-Book and Guide to Hancock, Michigan by A. H. Holland (1887)

The Americanization of the Finns by John Wargelin (1924)

The Beautiful in Time by F. X. Clifford (1949)
> subtitle: *Poems by F. X. Clifford*

Beyond the Boundaries by Larry Lankton (1997)
> subtitle: *Life and Landscape at the Lake Superior Copper Mines, 1840-1875*

Big Louie by Wilbert B. Maki (1989)
> subtitle: *Copper Country Giant*

Biographical Record by the Biographical Publishing Company (1903)
> subtitle: *Biographical Sketches of Leading Citizens of Houghton, Baraga and Marquette Counties, Michigan*

Challenge Accepted by Gary Kaunonen (2010)
> subtitle: *A Finnish Immigrant Response to Industrial America in Michigan's Copper Country*

Charter and Ordinances of the Village of Hancock by the Common Council (1901)

Church of the Resurrection Sesquicentennial Celebration published by Church of the Resurrection (2011)
> subtitle: *150 Years of Worship 1861-2011 Hancock, Michigan*

Copper Country Homecoming & Old Settler's Ball edited by Barb Herveat (2004)

Copper Country Postcards by Nancy Ann Sanderson (2005)
> subtitle: *A View of the Past from the Keweenaw Peninsula*

Dear Uncle translated by Raymond W. Wargelin (1984)
> subtitle: *Letters by J. K. Nikander and Other Pioneer Pastors*

East Hancock Revisited by Eleanor A. Alexander (1984)
> subtitle: *History of a Neighborhood Circa 1880-1920*

Exploring Michigan's Historic Copper Country by Celeste Haapala (2011)

The Faith of the Finns edited by Ralph J. Jalkanen (1972)
> subtitle: *Historical Perspectives on the Finnish Lutheran Church in America*

The Finn Factor in American Labor, Culture and Society by Carl Ross (1977)

Finns in Michigan by Gary Kaunonen (2009)

The Finns in North America edited by Ralph J. Jalkanen (1969)
> subtitle: *A Social Symposium*

From The Peninsula South by Sandra Seaton Michel (1980)
> subtitle: *The Story of Detroit & Northern Savings*

Gloria Dei Lutheran Church: Dedication published by Gloria Dei Lutheran Church (1970)

A Guide to Michigan's Historic Keweenaw Copper District by Lawrence J. Molloy (2011)
> subtitle: *Photographs, Maps, and Tours of the Keweenaw — Past and Present*

HANCOCK 1863 - 2013

Hancock Publications

Hancock by Wilbert B. Maki (1984)
    subtitle: *A Mosaic of Memories*

Hancock, Michigan Centennial: 1863-1963 edited by Gordon G. Barkell (1963)

Hancock, Michigan Remembered Volume I by Clarence J. Monette (1982)

Hancock, Michigan Remembered Volume II: Churches of Hancock by Clarence J.
    Monette (1985)

Hancock's City Centennial Book by Hancock's St. Patrick's Day Committee (2003)
    subtitle: *A Glimpse of Life in 1903*

History of the Diocese of Sault Ste. Marie and Marquette Vol. II by Rev. Antoine
    Ivan Rezek (1907)

History of the Finns in Michigan by Armas K. E. Holmio (2001)

History of the Hancock Public Schools by Wilbert B. Maki (1995)
    subtitles: *Where Futures are Formed; Echoes of a One-Room School*

A History of the Northern Peninsula of Michigan and its People by Alvah L. Sawyer (1911)

History of the Upper Peninsula of Michigan by The Western Historical Company (1883)

Hollowed Ground by Larry Lankton (2010)
    subtitle: *Copper Mining and Community Building on Lake Superior,
    1840s-1990s*

Houghton County: 1870-1920 by Richard E. Taylor (2006)

Houghton County's Streetcars and Electric Park by Clarence J. Monette (2001)

Kirkollinen Kalenteri published annually by the Finnish Evangelical Lutheran
    Church (1908-1981)

Memorial Record of the Northern Peninsula of Michigan by The Lewis Publishing
    Company (1895)

Michigan by Willis Frederick Dunbar (1965)
    subtitle: *A History of the Wolverine State*

Michiganin Kuparialue ja suomalaiset siirtolaiset by Juuso Hirvonen (1920)

Mine Towns by Alison K. Hoagland (2010)
    subtitle: *Buildings for Workers in Michigan's Copper Country*

Old Bottles and Jugs of Michigan's Copper Country by Copper Country Bottle
    Collectors (1978)

Old Reliable by Larry D. Lankton and Charles K. Hyde (1982)
    subtitle: *an Illustrated History of the Quincy Mining Company*

Ordinances of the City of Hancock, Michigan compiled by C. O. Oliver (1921)

Picturing the Past by Deborah K. Frontiera and Karen S. Johnson (2013)
    subtitle: *Finlandia University, 1896 to 2013*

Quincy Mining Company Hancock, Michigan · Mine · Mill · Smelter · Community
    published by The Copper Press
    subtitle: *A Look at the Architecture and Communities of the Quincy
    Mining Company*

Raittiuskansan Kalenteri published annually by the Temperance Society (1897-1972)

Rebels on the Range by Arthur W. Thurner (1984)
>   subtitle: *The Michigan Copper Miners' Strike of 1913-1914*

Reflections of the Hancock Copper Mine by Wilbert B. Maki (1982)

Reflections of the Hancock Fire Department by Wilbert B. Maki (1998)
>   subtitles: *Tragic Village Fire of 1869; Historic Landmark Fires*
>   *(Bucket Brigades to Fire Engines)*

Reminiscences of the Streetcar (1900-1932) by Wilbert B. Maki (1990s)

Sakari and Josephine Lassila and Their Descendants, Hancock, Michigan published by
>   J. W. Burlingame (1999)

The Sandstone Architecture of the Lake Superior Region by Kathryn Bishop Eckert (1982)

Seasons of Faith by Angela S. Johnson (2006)
>   subtitle: *A walk through the history of the Roman Catholic Diocese of*
>   *Marquette 1900-2000*

Sneakers Tours the Quincy Steam Hoist by Jim Lowell (2008)

A Souvenir in Photogravure of the Upper Peninsula of Michigan by W. E.
>   Steckbauer (1900)
>   subtitle: *Calumet, Red Jacket, Laurium, Houghton, Hancock, Lake Linden, Etc.*

The Story of the Suomi Synod by Jacob W. Heikkinen (1985)
>   subtitle: *The Finnish Evangelical Lutheran Church of America, 1890-1962:*
>   *"An Unquenchable Fire"*

Strangers and Sojourners by Arthur W. Thurner (1994)
>   subtitle: *A History of Michigan's Keweenaw Peninsula*

Suomi College 1896-1996 and beyond by Timo Koskinen (1996)
>   subtitle: *A Century of Opportunity: Centennial Book*

Visions to Keep by Sandra Seaton Michel (1990)
>   subtitle: *The D&N Story*

A Visitor's Guide to the Historic Quincy Mine by Lawrence J. Molloy (2007)

The Way It Was edited by Ralph J. Jalkanen (1990)
>   subtitle: *Memories of the Suomi Synod*

The Working Folks Bank by Superior National Bank & Trust Company (1990)
>   subtitle: *A History of Superior National Bank's First Century of Service,*
>   *1890-1990*

Also see:

A Brief List of Publications Pertaining to Copper Country History compiled by Clarence J. Monette (1979) available at the Portage Lake District Library

Copper Country in Print: 1843-1968 Bibliography compiled by Allen Good available at the Michigan Technological University Archives and Copper Country Historical Collections

There are several publications available that focus on individuals included in *Hidden Gems and Towering Tales: A Hancock, Michigan Anthology*. Some are mentioned above; others contain scant information on Hancock. Among this latter group the Hancock Sesquicentennial Committee recommends:

Biographical Sketch of the Life of the Late Samuel Worth Hill by Susan A. Hill (1894)
Edward Steichen: Lives in Photography by Todd Brandow and William A. Ewing (2008)
The Family of Man created by Edward Steichen; prologue by Carl Sandburg (1955)
      subtitle: *The greatest photographic exhibition of all time — 503 pictures from 68 countries*
A Great & Glorious Romance by Helga Sandburg (1978)
      subtitle: *The Story of Carl Sandburg and Lilian Steichen*
The Pewabic Pottery by Lillian Myers Pear (1976)
      subtitle: *A History of Its Products and Its People*
The Poet and the Dream Girl edited by Margaret Sandburg (1987)
      subtitle: *The Love Letters of Lilian Steichen & Carl Sandburg*
Steichen by Penelope Niven (1997)
      subtitle: *A Biography*
Steichen's Legacy edited with text by Joanna Steichen (2000)
      subtitle: *Photographs, 1895-1973*

Glenn Anderson has been Hancock's city manager since 1996. Glenn and his wife Mary Lou have three children, Stacy, Jacki, and Glenn. They reside at 740 Lake Avenue.

HANCOCK 1863 · 2013

Hancock Sesquicentennial Committee

Roland Burgan is a retired local radio and television broadcaster. He currently serves as a photojournalist for the City of Hancock website. Roland and his wife Mary have lived in Hancock since 1970. They reside at 2161 Jasberg Street.

Charles Eshbach is an author, publisher, photographer, conservationist, and wilderness guide, all while living in his most favorite place on Earth, the Keweenaw. Charlie and his wife Diane reside in Portage Township, Michigan.

Jack Eberhard has owned and operated Hancock's Book Concern Printers since 1984. He raised three sons, Kyle, Sean, and Sam. Jack resides at 302 Vivian Street.

Robert Grame is a designer and educator. He is an associate professor of Graphic Design in the International School of Art & Design at Finlandia University. Robert and his family reside in Houghton, Michigan.

John S. Haeussler is an academic researcher. He has lived in Hancock since 2007 and has been a member of the Hancock City Council since 2010. John, his wife Megan, and their children Maggie and Jack reside at 1203 Portage Drive.

Mary Pekkala is a retired vice president of Superior National Bank & Trust. Mary is a lifelong resident of Hancock and she is active in community affairs, particularly those related to Finnish heritage. She resides at 2008 St. Ann Circle.

Rob Roy is a retired insurance and real estate agent and Fine Arts instructor at Suomi College. Rob is a lifelong resident of Hancock and he is active in community affairs. Rob and his wife Mary reside at 312 Harris Avenue.

Editor

Laura Mahon is a freelance editor and community volunteer. She resides with her fiancé Jon-Paul Suchoski and their daughter Jayden at 934 Jennings Avenue.

Contributing Authors

Susan Burack is a member of the Houghton County Planning Commission, a former member of the Hancock City Council, and a community activist and volunteer. A born and bred Yankee and graduate of Bennington College, she has lived in Hancock since 1986. Susan resides in the Scott Building.

Mark Dennis is the director of O'Neill-Dennis Funeral Home, which has been in continuous operation for nearly 100 years. He is a graduate of the University of Minnesota and he has been a member of the Hancock Volunteer Fire Department since 1986. Mark and his wife Joy have three sons and six grandchildren. They reside at 214 Hancock Street.

HANCOCK 1863 · 2013

Additional Contributors

Corbin Eddy is a Catholic priest who served as pastor and seminary professor in Ottawa, Ontario, Canada, and Baltimore, Maryland. A native of the Copper Country, Corbin moved to Hancock upon his retirement in 2007. He resides at 624 Lake Avenue.

David Mac Frimodig graduated from Michigan Tech and retired from a career with the Michigan Department of Natural Resources. He was an active member of the Keweenaw County Historical Society and the Fort Wilkins Natural History Association and authored several publications including *Keweenaw Character*. Mac died in 1995. His widow, Kitti, resides in Laurium, Michigan.

Zach Hope graduated from Hancock Central High School in 2003. He has a degree in writing from Ithaca College and currently is a graduate student researching fish migration and watershed connectivity. Zach resides in Portland, Maine.

Karen S. Johnson is executive director of Communications at Finlandia University, where she has been employed since 2004. Karen is originally from Royal Oak, Michigan, and currently resides in South Range, Michigan, with her four cats.

Jeremie R. Moore is an avid historian and has lived in Hancock since 2006. He has been a member of the Hancock Volunteer Fire Department since 2009 and the Hancock City Council since 2010. Jeremie, his wife Jill, and their children Kaitlyn and Kyleigh reside at 914 Hill Street.

William H. Mulligan, Jr. is a professor of History at Murray State University. He is the MSU Alumni Association's Distinguished Researcher for 2012-13. He has degrees from Assumption College and Clark University and he previously taught at Michigan Tech. Bill was born in Brooklyn, New York, and currently resides in Murray, Kentucky.

Philip N. Parks is a retired professor of Physics at Michigan Tech. Phil and his wife Judy have lived in Hancock since 1969. They raised three children, Norman, Coleen, and Evan, all graduates of Hancock Central High School. Phil and Judy reside at 1228 Minnesota Street.

Don Roy is a retired security officer. He is a lifelong resident of the Copper Country and he is active as a local photographer. Don resides in Houghton, Michigan.

Marty Schendel is president of the alumni association for Hancock's Gamma Alpha chapter of the Phi Kappa Tau fraternity. He lived at 1209 West Quincy Street from 1981 to 1985. Marty and his wife Susan have three children, Chris, Lauren, and Danielle. They reside in Canton, Michigan.

Tim Seppanen manages a construction office in Hancock. He is a Michigan Tech graduate, military history buff, and battlefield tramper. Tim, his wife Michelle, and their daughter Aurora reside in Alston, Michigan.

Stephen Alan Smith was born in Detroit, raised in Ann Arbor, and has lived in Hancock since 1985, thus crossing historic paths with Mary Chase Perry Stratton in all three Michigan cities. He is a teacher at Hancock Central High School. Stephen and his wife Ruth Ann reside at 209 Center Street.

Kristin Vichich was born in Hancock and grew up at 1012 (now 1020) Ethel Avenue. She works with medical records for Humana Insurance. Kristin resides in De Pere, Wisconsin, with her sucker fish, Frank, and three surprisingly hearty African violets.

Contributing Designers
Kelsey Norz is a student in the International School of Art & Design at Finlandia University where she studies graphic design.

Audrey Small is a student in the International School of Art & Design at Finlandia University where she studies graphic design.

Additional support provided by Ben Miller, Haley Neri, and Mike Simila, students in the International School of Art & Design at Finlandia University.

In appreciation of their contribution to the publication, the Hancock Sesquicenten-
nial Committee and authors thank Theresa Alafita, Eleanor Alexander, Jacki Anderson,
Stacy Anderson, Bob Backon, Tim Bausano, Tony Bausano, Jim Beran, John Bosio, Mary
Seaton Brush, Jack Condon, Trent Cunard, Ed Duda, Mikki Gagnon, Deb Gardner, Mike
Gemignani, Jack Haeussler, Maggie Haeussler, Megan Haeussler, Jim Hainault, Dave
Hermanson, Kevin Hodur, Dave Jaehnig, Gail Johnson, Kurt Johnson, Manu Kerola, Joe
Kirkish, Julie Kloss, Mike Lahti, Bill Laitila, Mitch Lake, Doug Lancour, Larry Lankton,
John Lawton, Michael Lorence, Josephine Marshall, Chris Mason, Bob Mikesch, Larry
Molloy, Paul Nelson, Jane Nordberg, Steph Olsson, Bob O'Neill, Rob O'Neill, Jeffery
Primeau, Dana Richter, Francis Roberts, Richard Salani, Judy Schaefer, Bill Schoos,
Ken Seaton, Reverend Sister Laurian Seeber, Mike Shanahan, Luci Sintkowski, Rob
Sintkowski, Marty Smith, Bob Stebler, Dick Storm, Virginia Sullivan, Jeff Thiel, Mary
Tuisku, Judy Usitalo, John Vaara, Tom Vichich, Vicky Vichich, Pete Wickley, Dave
Wiitanen, and Mark Wilcox.

HANCOCK 1863 - 2013

Acknowledgments

We also express our gratitude to the Archives of Michigan; Artists Rights Society (J'Aimee
Cronin and Hannah Rhadigan); Aurelia Sultan; Barre (MA) Historical Society (Audrey
Stevens); Bentley Historical Library, University of Michigan (Diana Bachman and
Marilyn McNitt); Briscoe Center for American History, University of Texas at Austin
(Sarah Traugott); Bureau of Health Professions, State of Michigan; Carnegie Museum
(Elise Nelson, Bob Drake, and Deb Mann); Carousel Research (Laurie Platt Winfrey);
Carp Lake Township Library (Wanda Tessmer); City of Hancock (Karen Haischer, Beth
Fredianelli, and Tina Posega); Columbia University (Mathew Bolton and Bill Santin);
Church of the Resurrection (Fr. Brian Gerber and Jen Norkol); Crow Wing County (MN)
Auditor-Treasurer's office; *Daily Mining Gazette* (Michael B. Scott); Elm River
Township (Shawn Hagan, Lisa Saatio, and Bob Sibilsky); Estate of Edward Steichen;
Fairfield Citizen (Jim Doody); Finlandia University (Bonnie Holland and Fred Knoch);
Finlandia University Finnish American Historical Archive and Museum; First United
Methodist Church; Fontbonne University (Elizabeth Hise Brennan and Jim Visser);
General Federation of Women's Clubs - Michigan (Donna Brown); Glad Tidings
Assembly of God; Gloria Dei Lutheran Church; Hancock Business & Professionals
Association (Jen Burkhouse); Hancock Housing Commission (Gail Ross); Hancock Public
Schools (Monica Healy and Sheri Aldrich); Harvard University (Robin Carlaw, Emily
Carson, Virginia Hunt, Jennifer Jacobsen, Megan Sniffin-Marinoff, and Seth Williams);
Houghton County Arena; Houghton County Clerk and Register of Deeds' offices (Mary
Schoos, Pat Janke, Mary Ann Krug, Susan Lewis, Mary Sivonen, and Beverly Smith);
Houghton County Commissioners, 2012; Houghton County Historical Society (Kristy
Walden and Gloria Walli); Houghton County Treasurer's office (Kathy Beattie, Judy
Carne, Lisa Mattila, and Karen Semmens); Houghton-Keweenaw County Genealogical
Society (Avis West); Houghton-Portage Township Schools (Kim Maki); Keweenaw
County Clerk's office (Roxanne Karrio); Keweenaw National Historical Park (Jeremiah
Mason); Library of Congress; Lone Star Pictures; Magnum Photos (Michael Shulman);

Marquette County Clerk's office; McGill University (Julie Fortier, Chris Lyons, and Theresa Rowat); *Michigan History*; Michigan Legislative Council Facilities Agency (Steve Benkovsky); Michigan Technological University Archives and Copper Country Historical Collections (Erik Nordberg, Beth Russell, Megan Dirickson, Sawyer Newman, Annette Perkowski, and Allyse Staehler); Montana Historical Society (Tammy Ryan); Mu Kappa Mu; Museo Picasso Málaga (Juana María Suárez); Museum of Modern Art; National Archives and Records Administration; *Northwestern Mining Journal*; *Old Cardboard* (Lyman Hardeman); Paramount Pictures; Pewabic Pottery (Christina Devlin, Robert-David Jones, and Hanne F. Nielsen); Phi Kappa Tau (Steve Hartman); Portage Health (Victor Harrington and volunteer greeters); Portage Lake District Library (Judy Foster, Mary Hickey, Dave Karnosky, Rachele Lambert, Deb Ragan, and Wendy Sharp); Portage Township; Quincy Mine Hoist Association (Glenda Bierman); Rotary Club of Hancock; Ruggles Lane (MA) Elementary School; Seaton family; Sisters of St. Joseph of Carondelet (Sister Jane Behlmann and Sister Mary Sharon Jones); (former) State (MI) Representative Matt Huuki's office (Joy Brewer); State (MI) Representative Steve Lindberg; John H. Twist; United States Postal Service (Jennifer Lynch); University of Montreal (William Raillant-Clark); Van Pelt and Opie Library, Michigan Technological University (Amanda Binoniemi, Jon Curtis, Nathan Eilola, and Marisa Glazier); Vassar College (Diane Hackenbrock, Ronald D. Patkus, and Dean M. Rogers); VEGAP (Eva Mª Hernández Martín); Victoria University Archives (Ken Wilson); and, Zion Lutheran Church.

The Hancock Sesquicentennial Committee extends its gratitude to Gordon G. Barkell, editor of Hancock's centennial publication, who passed away in 2012.

We apologize to anyone who has been inadvertently omitted.

HANCOCK 1863 - 2013

Image Credits

Cover	Edward Steichen, 1959; photo by Philippe Halsman. Courtesy of Magnum Photos.
Inside	Bird's-eye view of Hancock, 1873. Courtesy of the City of Hancock.
Pages 8-11	Scenes from bird's-eye view of Hancock, 1873. Courtesy of the City of Hancock.
Page 13	Big Louie Moilanen. Courtesy of Michigan Technological University Archives and Copper Country Historical Collections.
Page 15	Hervey C. Parke. Courtesy of the City of Hancock.
Page 17	Abraham Lincoln, 1863; photo by Alexander Gardner. Public domain.
Page 19	Daniel Ruggles; photo by Mathew Brady. Public domain.
Page 20	Ruggles' Battery; photo by Tim Seppanen. Courtesy of Tim Seppanen.
Page 23	Samuel W. Hill; photo by Bain News Service. Courtesy of the Library of Congress, LC-DIG-ggbain-22254.
Page 25	Mary Chase Perry working in Stable-Studio, Detroit. Courtesy of Pewabic Pottery Archives.
Page 28	Mary Chase Perry demonstrating Revelation Kilns. Courtesy of Pewabic Pottery Archives. Early example of Pewabic Pottery. Courtesy of Pewabic Pottery Archives. Pewabic House, birthplace of Mary Chase Perry. Courtesy of Pewabic Pottery Archives.
Page 29	Mary Chase Perry Stratton at Pewabic Pottery, Detroit. Courtesy of Pewabic Pottery Archives. Detroit Public Library. Courtesy of Pewabic Pottery Archives. Crypt Church, National Shrine of the Immaculate Conception, Washington, D.C. Courtesy of Pewabic Pottery Archives.
Page 31	Most Holy Redeemer Church, Detroit. Courtesy of Pewabic Pottery Archives. Guardian Building, Detroit. Courtesy of Pewabic Pottery Archives. Mary Chase Perry Stratton. Public domain.
Page 33	Reverend J. K. Nikander; photo by C. A. Silfven. Courtesy of the Finlandia University Finnish American Historical Archive and Museum.
Page 35	Porvoo Cathedral; photo by Manu Kerola. Courtesy of Manu Kerola.
Page 37	John D. Ryan; photo by Harris & Ewing. Courtesy of the Library of Congress, LC-DIG-hec-19237.
Page 42	Reverend Edward Jacker. Courtesy of Michigan Technological University Archives and Copper Country Historical Collections.
Page 45	Ryan Hall, Fontbonne University, St. Louis; photo by Jim Visser. Courtesy of Fontbonne University. Ryan home, 3 E 78th Street, Manhattan; photo by Jeffery Primeau. Courtesy of Jeffery Primeau.
Page 46	John D. Ryan; photo by Bain News Service. Courtesy of the Library of Congress, LC-DIG-ggbain-26035.

Page 107   Verna Hillie tobacco cards, 1936 Aurelia Sultan Filmsterne series.
            Public domain.
Page 108   John Wayne and Verna Hillie in *The Star Packer*, 1934.
            Courtesy of Lone Star Pictures.
Page 109   Harpo Marx and Verna Hillie in *Duck Soup*, 1933.
            Courtesy of Paramount Pictures.
            Randolph Scott, Verna Hillie, and Vince Barnett in *Man of the Forest*, 1933.
            Courtesy of Paramount Pictures.
Page 110   Rod Paavola, 1960. Public domain.
Page 111   Paul Coppo, 1960; photo by Charles Eshbach. Courtesy of Charles Eshbach.
            Bruce Riutta. Courtesy of Houghton County Arena.
Page 112   Mary Seaton, 1970s. Courtesy of the Seaton family.
Page 113   Mary Seaton. Courtesy of Mary Seaton Brush.